These primers on Jonathan Edwards  passion for God—provide an excelle unto God. And they help the rest of majesty of our Savior. We owe a grea Douglas Sweeney for making Edwards and his vision of God so accessible to the rest of us thirsty pilgrims.

> —**Thabiti Anyabwile**, Pastor of First Baptist Church of
> Grand Cayman, Cayman Islands

Everyone says Jonathan Edwards is important. Quite frankly, however, his writing style is pretty dense by contemporary standards, so few pastors and other Christian leaders have invested much time reading him. This new series tackles the problem. Here is the kernel of much of Edwards's thought in eminently accessible form.

> —**D. A. Carson**, Research Professor of New Testament,
> Trinity Evangelical Divinity School

In *The Essential Edwards Collection*, Owen Strachan and Doug Sweeney point with knowledge and excitement to clear and searching sections that illuminate God's truth and search our hearts. In this collection, Edwards is introduced to a new generation of readers. His concerns are made our concerns. This is a worthy effort and I pray that God will bless it.

> —**Mark Dever**, Senior Pastor, Capitol Hill Baptist
> Church, Washington, DC

I am deeply impressed with the vision that has brought together this splendid library of volumes to introduce Jonathan Edwards to a new generation. Owen Strachan and Douglas Sweeney have provided an incredible service by making the often challenging writings of America's greatest theologian accessible for seasoned theologians, pastors, and students alike with their five-volume *Essential Edwards Collection*. This series is properly titled the "essential collection."

> —**David S. Dockery**, President, Union University

This series is a fantastic introduction to the heart, mind, and ministry of the greatest theologian America has ever produced.
> —**Mark Driscoll**, Pastor of Mars Hill Church, President of the Acts 29 Church Planting Network

Jonathan Edwards was a preacher of the Word, a pastor of souls, a philosopher of first rank, and the greatest theologian America has ever produced. In this wonderful new anthology of Edwards's writings, the great Puritan saint lives again. I can think of no better tonic for our transcendence-starved age than the writings of Edwards. But beware: reading this stuff can change your life forever!
> —**Timothy George**, Founding Dean of Beeson Divinity School of Samford University

Let Strachan and Sweeney serve as your guides through the voluminous writings of America's greatest theologian. They have been shaped by his godly counsel and moved by his passion for Christ. By God's grace, Edwards can do the same for you. Start your journey with *The Essential Edwards Collection.*
> —**Collin Hansen**, Author of *Young, Restless, Reformed*

Owen Strachan and Douglas Sweeney have done us all a great service by remixing and reloading the teaching of Jonathan Edwards for a new generation. They do more than introduce us to his writing: they show us how his biblical teaching relates to a modern world and leave us hungry for more. I am very impressed and very grateful for *The Essential Edwards Collection.*
> —**Joshua Harris**, Senior Pastor of Covenant Life Church

From a course he taught at Yale and in personal friendship, Doug Sweeney has taught me much about Edwards. Possessing a command of the academic field, he and Owen Strachan nevertheless write this collection with pastoral concern, showing the relevance of Edwards for our Christian faith and practice today. It's a rare combination of gifts and insights that Sweeney and Strachan bring to this task.

—**Michael Horton**, J. Gresham Machen Professor of Systematic Theology and Apologetics, Westminster Theological Seminary California

When it comes to Jonathan Edwards's writing, where does an average reader (like me!) begin? Right here, with *The Essential Edwards Collection.* Strachan and Sweeney provide a doorway into the life and teaching of one of the church's wisest theologians. The authors have also included notes of personal application to help us apply the life and teaching of Edwards to our own lives. I've read no better introduction to Jonathan Edwards.

—**C. J. Mahaney**, President of Sovereign Grace Ministries

Why hasn't this been done before? *The Essential Edwards Collection* is now essential reading for the serious-minded Christian. Doug Sweeney and Owen Strachan have written five excellent and accessible introductions to America's towering theological genius—Jonathan Edwards. They combine serious scholarship with the ability to make Edwards and his theology come alive for a new generation. *The Essential Edwards Collection* is a great achievement and a tremendous resource. I can't think of a better way to gain a foundational knowledge of Edwards and his lasting significance.

—**R. Albert Mohler Jr.**, President of The Southern Baptist Theological Seminary

A great resource! Edwards continues to speak, and this series of books is an excellent means to hear Jonathan Edwards again live and clear. Pure gold; be wise and invest in it!

—**Dr. Josh Moody**, Senior Pastor, College Church in Wheaton.

You hold in your hands a unique resource: a window into the life and thought of Jonathan Edwards, a man whose life was captured by God for the gospel of Jesus Christ. In these pages you'll not only learn about Edwards, but you'll be able to hear him speak in his own words. This winsome and accessible introduction is now the first thing I'd recommend for those who want to know more about America's greatest pastor-theologian.

—**Justin Taylor**, Managing Editor, ESV Study Bible

Jonathan Edwards is surely one of the most influential theologians of the eighteenth century. Now, at last, we have a wide-ranging and representative sample of his work published in an attractive, accessible and, most important of all, readable form. The authors are to be commended for the work they have put into this set and I hope it will become an important feature of the library of many pastors and students of the Christian faith.

—**Carl R. Trueman**, Academic Dean, Westminster Theological Seminary

JONATHAN EDWARDS
on TRUE CHRISTIANITY

The Essential
EDWARDS
Collection

OWEN STRACHAN *and* DOUGLAS SWEENEY

MOODY PUBLISHERS
CHICAGO

© 2010 by
OWEN STRACHAN
DOUGLAS SWEENEY

All rights reserved. No part of this book may be reproduced in any form without permission in writing from the publisher, except in the case of brief quotations embodied in critical articles or reviews.

All Scripture quotations, except those that appear in original source material, are
taken from *The Holy Bible, English Standard Version.* Copyright © 2000; 2001 by
Crossway Bibles, a division of Good News Publishers. Used by permission. All rights
reserved.

Scripture quotations marked KJV are taken from the King James Version.

All websites listed herein are accurate at the time of publication, but may change in
the future or cease to exist. The listing of website references and resources does not
imply publisher endorsement of the site's entire contents. Groups, corporations, and
organizations are listed for informational purposes, and listing does not imply publisher endorsement of their activities.

Editor: Christopher Reese
Interior Design: Ragont Design
Cover Design: Gearbox

Library of Congress Cataloging-in-Publication Data

Strachan, Owen.
    Jonathan Edwards on true Christianity / Owen Strachan and Douglas Sweeney.
        p. cm. — (The essential Edwards collection)
    Includes bibliographical references.
    ISBN 978-0-8024-2460-0
    1. Edwards, Jonathan, 1703-1758. 2. Commitment to the church.
    3. Christian life. I. Sweeney, Douglas A. II. Title.
    BV4520.S68 2010
    248—dc22

                                                              2009040813

We hope you enjoy this book from Moody Publishers. Our goal is to provide high-
quality, thought-provoking books and products that connect truth to your real needs
and challenges. For more information on other books and products written and produced from a biblical perspective, go to www.moodypublishers.com or write to:

Moody Publishers
820 N. LaSalle Boulevard
Chicago, IL 60610

1 3 5 7 9 10 8 6 4 2

Printed in the United States of America

The Essential Edwards Collection

Jonathan Edwards: Lover of God

Jonathan Edwards on Beauty

Jonathan Edwards on Heaven and Hell

Jonathan Edwards on the Good Life

Jonathan Edwards on True Christianity

CONCORDIA UNIVERSITY LIBRARY
PORTLAND, OR 97211

OS

To Mark Dever,
whose Edwardsean ministry has led many
to experience the delights of authentic faith

DS

To Lou Korom,
an ever-faithful evangelist, who has helped
so many others understand true Christianity

Contents

Abbreviations of Works Cited

The following shortened forms of books by or about Jonathan Edwards are used in the text to indicate the source of quotations.

Barna, George. *Today's Pastors: A Revealing Look at What Pastors Are Saying About Themselves, Their Peers and the Pressures They Face.* Ventura, CA: Regal, 1999.
Cited as "Barna" in the text.

Christianity Today. "Willow Creek Repents?" CT Blog, October 18, 2007.
Cited as "CT" in the text.

Guinness, Os. *Fit Bodies Fat Minds: Why Evangelicals Don't Think and What to Do About It.* Grand Rapids: Baker, 1994.
Cited as "Guinness" in the text.

Kimnach, Wilson H., Kenneth P. Minkema, and Douglas A. Sweeney, eds. *The Sermons of Jonathan Edwards: A Reader.* New Haven: Yale Univ. Press, 1999.
Cited as "Kimnach" in the text.

Lindsay, D. Michael and George Gallup. *Surveying the Religious Landscape: Trends in U.S. Beliefs*. Harrisburg, PA: Morehouse Group, 2000.
Cited as "Lindsay" in the text.

Smith, Christian. *Soul Searching: The Religious and Spiritual Lives of American Teenagers*. New York: Oxford University Press, 2005.
Cited as "Smith" in the text.

Stark, Rodney. *What Americans Really Believe*. Waco: Baylor University Press, 2008.
Cited as "Stark" in the text.

Wells, David. *Above All Earthly Pow'rs: Christ in a Postmodern World*. Grand Rapids: Eerdmans, 2005.
Cited as "Above All Earthly Pow'rs" in the text.

_____. *The Courage to Be Protestant: Truth-lovers, Marketers, and Emergents in the Postmodern World*. Grand Rapids: Eerdmans, 2008.
Cited as "Courage to Be Protestant" in the text.

Books in the Yale University Press *Works of Jonathan Edwards* series

In the text, the volumes are listed in the following format: (*Works* 1, 200). The "1" refers to the series volume; the "200" refers to the page number in the given volume.

Edwards, Jonathan. *Freedom of the Will*, ed. Paul Ramsey, *The Works of Jonathan Edwards*, vol. 1. New Haven: Yale, 1957.

_____. *Religious Affections*, ed. John Smith, *The Works of Jonathan Edwards*, vol. 2. New Haven: Yale, 1959.

_____. *The Great Awakening*, ed. C. C. Goen, *The Works of Jonathan Edwards*, vol. 4. New Haven: Yale, 1972.

_____. *The Life of David Brainerd*, ed. Norman Pettit, *The Works of Jonathan Edwards*, vol. 7. New Haven: Yale, 1984.

_____. *Ecclesiastical Writings*, ed. David Hall, *The Works of Jonathan Edwards*, vol. 12. New Haven: Yale, 1994.

_____. *Sermons and Discourses, 1723–1729*, ed. Kenneth E. Minkema, *The Works of Jonathan Edwards*, vol. 14. New Haven: Yale, 1997.

_____. *Sermons and Discourses, 1734–1738*, ed. M. X. Lesser, *The Works of Jonathan Edwards*, vol. 19. New Haven: Yale, 2001.

_____. *Sermons and Discourses, 1743–1758*, ed. Mark Valeri, *The Works of Jonathan Edwards*, vol. 25. New Haven: Yale, 2006.

Jonathan Edwards, a God-Entranced Man

*W*hen I was in seminary, a wise professor told me that besides the Bible I should choose one great theologian and apply myself throughout life to understanding and mastering his thought. This way I would sink at least one shaft deep into reality, rather than always dabbling on the surface of things. I might come to know at least one system with which to bring other ideas into fruitful dialogue. It was good advice.

The theologian I have devoted myself to is Jonathan Edwards. All I knew of Edwards when I went to seminary was that he preached a sermon called "Sinners in the Hands of an Angry God," in which he said something about hanging over hell by a slender thread. My first real encounter with Edwards was when I read his "Essay on the Trinity" and wrote a paper on it for church history.

It had a lasting effect on me. It gave me a conceptual framework with which to grasp, in part, the meaning of saying God is three in one. In brief, there is God the Father, the fountain of being, who from all eternity has had a perfectly clear and distinct image and idea of himself; and this image is the eternally begotten Son. Between this Son and Father there flows a stream of infinitely vigorous love and perfectly holy communion; and this is God the Spirit. God's Image of God and God's Love of God are so full of God that they are fully divine Persons, and not less.

After graduation from college, and before my wife and I took off for graduate work in Germany, we spent some restful days on a small farm in Barnesville, Georgia. Here I had another encounter with Edwards. Sitting on one of those old-fashioned two-seater swings in the backyard under a big hickory tree, with pen in hand, I read *The Nature of True Virtue*. I have a long entry in my journal from July 14, 1971, in which I try to understand, with Edwards's help, why a Christian is obligated to forgive wrongs when there seems to be a moral law in our hearts that cries out against evil in the world.

Later, when I was in my doctoral program in Germany, I encountered Edwards's *Dissertation Concerning the End for Which God Created the World*. I read it in a pantry in our little apartment in Munich. The pantry was about 8 by 5 feet, a most unlikely place to read a book like the *Dissertation*. From my perspective now, I would say that if there were one book that captures the essence or wellspring of Edwards's theology, this would be it. Edwards's answer to the question of why God created the world is this: to emanate the fullness of His glory for His people to know, praise, and enjoy. Here is the heart of his theology in his own words:

> IT APPEARS THAT ALL that is ever spoken of in the Scripture as an ultimate end of God's works is included in that one phrase, *the glory of God.* In the creatures' knowing, esteeming, loving, rejoicing in and praising God, the glory of God is both exhibited and acknowledged; his fullness is received and returned. Here is both the *emanation* and *remanation.* The refulgence shines upon and into the creature, and is reflected back to the luminary. The beams of glory come from God, and are something of God and are refunded back again to their original. So that the whole is *of* God and *in* God, and *to* God, and God is the beginning, middle and end in this affair. (*Works* 8, 531)

That is the heart and center of Jonathan Edwards and, I believe, of the Bible too. That kind of reading can turn a pantry into a vestibule of heaven.

I am not the only person for whom Edwards continues to be a vestibule of heaven. I hear testimonies regularly that people have stumbled upon this man's work and had their world turned upside down. There are simply not many writers today whose mind and heart are God-entranced the way Edwards was. Again and again, to this very day his writings help me know that experience.

My prayer for *The Essential Edwards Collection* is that it will draw more people into the sway of Edwards's God-entranced worldview. I hope that many who start here, or continue here, will make their way to Edwards himself. Amazingly, almost everything he wrote is available on the Internet. And increasingly his works are available in affordable books. I am thankful that Owen Strachan and Douglas Sweeney share my conviction that every effort to point to Edwards, and through him to his God, is a worthy investment of our lives. May that be the outcome of these volumes.

John Piper
Pastor for Preaching and Vision
Bethlehem Baptist Church
Minneapolis, Minnesota

Jonathan Edwards and the Challenge of Nominal Christianity

*W*hat is a true Christian? What is the church?

Though these are fundamental questions, they often go unanswered in our current evangelical context. Oftentimes, we focus little on what actually makes a Christian a Christian and what makes a church a church. This has fed an age-old problem: nominal Christianity, or Christianity that exists in name only. If you have ever witnessed an ongoing pattern of half-hearted belief and weak action on the part of a professing Christian, you have seen the scandal of nominal Christianity.

Throughout history, pastors following the Bible have confronted this problem of nominalism, though few have addressed it with greater experience or insight than the eighteenth-century

Massachusetts pastor Jonathan Edwards. As we will see, Edwards dealt with nominal Christianity throughout his pastoral career and devoted many sermons and writings to the subject. Though he is sometimes presented as a hardboiled parson who relished belting out damnations, a careful study of the historical record and Edwards's writings shows that he was in fact a Christian man devoted to the cultivation of saving faith in spiritually fickle people. We will set Edwards in his context in the pages to come, shedding light on his shepherd's heart and his difficult circumstances.

But first, we will examine an era quite different from Edwards's—our own. In the first chapter, we seek to diagnose and understand the struggle of many Christians and churches with lukewarm faith. We reveal in the process that the problem of noncommittal Christianity did not end with Edwards. It not only survives, but thrives, in the current day.

From there, we will work through Edwards's personal acquaintance with uncommitted Christianity in chapter two. We'll look at how he defined true Christianity and his pastoral guidance on the matter in chapter three. We will see as we do so that the pastor's teaching, though addressed to an era quite different from our own, has eminent theological and practical relevance for our modern situation.

In chapter four, we will look briefly at two lives that embody Edwards's conception of true Christianity. In these two examples, we will find fresh impetus to pursue authentic spirituality, and discover that one need not be an evangelical superstar to do great things for good. We will conclude with chapter five by noting what Edwards's view of conversion led him to do in his own church, demonstrating that Edwards was no ivory-tower thinker, but a pastor who lived his convictions even to the bitter—but scripturally faithful—end. We will then suggest several major lessons and emphases we can pick up from Edwards and apply to the challenges of our day.

We interact extensively in *Jonathan Edwards on True Christianity* with the actual writing of Edwards. It will take a little time to get used to his style, but it is our belief that investing even a little effort in reading his writing will yield a huge spiritual payoff. We will mix in our commentary on his writing even as we sketch a general picture of his understanding of real Christianity. As we go, we will offer brief suggestions for application of his views that we hope will be of use to you in your personal reading or in the context of group study.

Though we both enjoy delving deeply into subjects like this one, we cannot cover every base in this book. The broader *Essential Edwards Collection* allows the reader to delve much deeper into his thinking and preaching, but we seek in *Jonathan Edwards on True Christianity* to bring to light an important emphasis of Edwards's ministry, one that few may recognize but all can profit from. We seek to make Edwards accessible to a wide audience. This book is intended for the uninitiated, but we hope and intend for it—and for this series—to be of use to pastors, students, church leaders, small groups, and many more besides. We want those who consider Edwards their "homeboy" as well as those who have never read a single word of his to profit from this material.

As we jump into the text, we will soon see that nominal Christianity, a considerable challenge today, has historic roots. By observing how Edwards handled this issue in his own time and ministry, we will find encouragement and a biblically grounded example to guide us as we confront the same challenge today.

CHAPTER ONE

The Contemporary Problem of Nominal Christianity

*F*ew things in the world speak to the soul with greater depth than a committed marriage relationship. When two people share love and cling to one another through decades of life, weathering trials, tragedies, and tense times, they offer the world an image of a greater reality.

But if the sweetness of true love easily moves us, the specter of half-hearted marital commitment equally raises our passions. Many of us have watched with sorrow and surprise as the covenants of many couples collapse. We have seen the story play out time and time again: the sweethearts everyone admires marry and raise adorable children in a happy home. Without warning, the marriage crumbles, often as a result of a spouse's unfaithfulness. Though everything seemed so perfect, we learn in the end that all was not well. There may have been sparks of true affection over the years, but ultimately, what looked like love was no love at all.

Relating Marriage and Faith

This situation parallels a matter of even greater significance: Christian faith. Just as marriage is not merely a slip of paper and a big ceremony, Christian faith is not merely a one-time confession of Christ and occasional church attendance. If we would reach heaven, if we would truly live by faith, we must be personally transformed by God such that we pursue Him, however imperfectly, on a constant basis. This, at base, is the nature of Christianity. Though still bearing sin, we fight for holiness and watch as God, over time, conforms us to the image of His Son. We back up our "profession"—our verbal commitment—to God by our lives, thus showing ourselves to be truly saved (see 1 John 1).

Unashamed sinners and passionate Christians form two clear scriptural groups. The Bible deals extensively with the unredeemed and the redeemed. But the Scripture also recognizes a third group. This group mirrors the half-hearted spouse discussed above: the lukewarm, interested but non-committal, nominal Christian who professes true faith but shows little evidence of it (nominal refers to "name," that is, a faith in name only). To this group the voices of Scripture also devote much attention. The prophets call Israel to stop wandering from God; Jesus Christ tells deeply frightening stories about those who pursue Him half-heartedly (see Matthew 13:1–23, for example); Revelation informs us that at the last judgment, the Lord will spew the lukewarm from His mouth (Revelation 3:16). In these and many other instances, the Scripture warns the nominal Christian of clear and present danger. We are not merely dealing with earthly situations here. On the matter of true Christianity, we are confronting matters of eternal consequence.

Nominal Christianity in Our Day

As we will see in the quotations and statistics that follow, lukewarm faith is alive and well in our evangelical churches. By studying this problem in its contemporary form, we prepare ourselves to enter Jonathan Edwards's world in coming chapters.

Nominal Christianity is a notoriously difficult problem to trace and spot. Like a transmittable illness, one knows it's out there, but one can't pinpoint exactly where. Two things are immediately clear, though: the state of maturity of many Christians is quite low, and many churches are failing to educate their people in the basics of Christianity.

Confused Beliefs

Pollsters D. Michael Lindsay and George Gallup conducted research several years ago that revealed alarming beliefs among a significant number of people who claim to be evangelical.

According to Lindsay and Gallup, of those claiming to be born again:

- 33% hold a pro-choice stance on abortion
- 26% believe in astrology
- 20% believe in reincarnation (Lindsay, 40)

Many of these people are likely in evangelical churches that ostensibly teach biblical doctrine, and yet they hold views on various spiritual and moral subjects that directly conflict with the biblical witness. If their beliefs conflict with true Christianity, it is likely that their lives conflict as well.

Deficient Living

In a study of members of prominent evangelical megachurches, Rodney Stark found the following data:

- ONLY 46% attend services weekly or more often
- Only 46% tithe
- Only 33% read the Bible daily (Stark, 47)

When Stark and his researchers asked the megachurch members the following question, *"How often in the last month did you participate in witnessing/sharing your faith with strangers?"*

the following percentage answered that they witnessed one or more times:

- All Conservative Protestants 44%
- All Liberal Protestants 19% (Stark, 25)

This could initially seem encouraging. When one considers, though, that more than half of all *conservative* Protestants, people who seemingly have a great concern for personal evangelism, did not share their faith even once in the month with an unbeliever, reality begins to sink in.

A recent survey by an evangelical megachurch backed up this conclusion. It revealed that a significant number of its members who self-identified as spiritually healthy—"close to Christ" and "Christ-centered" were the words used in the survey—also marked themselves as "spiritually stalled" and "dissatisfied." *Christianity Today* commented on the survey that "About a quarter of the 'stalled' segment and 63 percent of the 'dissatisfied' segment contemplated leaving the church." (CT) These findings come from a seemingly thriving church reaching many thousands of people each year.

It is true that all Christians sometimes feel "stalled" in their faith. Sin is a part of our lives, and it will not leave us until we reach the other side. But because of the vast number of members who described themselves in this way, these numbers do not indicate health in the church.

Biblical Illiteracy

In his book *Today's Pastors*, George Barna documents the disheartening results of his study of the biblical literacy or knowledge of many Christians. First, Barna found that just four out of ten Christians read their Bible on a weekly basis. Second, according to Barna:

> THOSE PEOPLE WHO DO READ will commit about one hour to Bible reading during the week. Those people actually will spend more time showering, commuting to and from work, watching television, reading the newspaper, eating meals or talking on the telephone. Obviously, the Bible is not a high priority in the lives of most people. (Barna, 48)

If we're still skeptical about the specter of listless Christianity, this statistic wakes us up. The decided minority of professing Christians who do crack the pages of the Word of God spend less time in it each week *than they do in the shower*.

David Wells, the eminent theologian and critic of evangelicalism, cites other Barna polls that show that a majority—52%—of evangelicals "reject the idea of original sin outright" (*Courage to Be Protestant*, 57). This means that a majority of professing believers simply reject one of the core doctrines of a Christian view of mankind altogether. Furthermore, Wells cites statistics that show that only 32% of professing evangelicals believe in absolutes in truth or morality (*Above All Earthly Pow'rs*, 93). These are the sort of statements we expect from outspoken unbelievers, not professing Christians.

The Problem of Pornography

The harmful effects of pornography are well-known. Yet the church, commissioned to be an outpost of holiness in a world of evil, has struggled mightily to help its members turn away from pornography. Some of the most discouraging data comes from pastors, those charged to lead congregations through holy lives. The following data comes from the Safe Families website (www.safe-families.org):

- 37% of pastors say pornography is a current struggle
- In another survey, over half of evangelical pastors admitted viewing pornography last year
- Of pastors who had visited a porn site, 53% had visited such sites "a few times" in the past year, and 18% visit sexually explicit sites between a couple of times a month and more than once a week

If the pastors of God's churches are struggling as mightily as these polls suggest, one wonders how church members, many of them far less spiritually mature than pastors, are faring in the fight against lust.

The Tragedy of Divorce

Other data indicate that the church is not only failing in its mission to be distinct and unique, but it is full of the same cultural sins that the world practices. In some cases, the church actually may be *surpassing* the world in its sins. In 1999, the Barna Group found that conservative evangelicals apparently divorce at a higher rate than non-Christians. The following figures comparing rates of divorce between Christians and non-Christians echo this shocking claim:

- Non–Denominational 34%
- Mainline Protestants 25%
- Atheists/Agnostics 21%

(www.associatedcontent.com)

This statistic paints an unflattering portrait of the state of Christian marriage. Of course, it needs to be qualified; one could point out here that professing Christians are more likely to marry than unbelievers and thus are more susceptible to divorce. One could also note that many conservative Christian theologians believe that divorce is allowed in some circumstances. With these points noted, though, it is clear that many Christians have bought into the American divorce culture. Rather than standing apart from the world in this area, many Christians mirror their unbelieving neighbors. In a society rapidly releasing itself from connection to Christian moral and theological thinking, many Christians are not even fighting the cultural tide, let alone stemming it. It is sweeping them away.

Sub-Christian Faith Among Young Adults

The lives and testimony of our children, though surely not ultimately dependent on the faith of parents, reveal with painful precision just how much faith makes its way into nominally Christian homes. Interviewers and researchers who have talked with hundreds of children of conservative Christian parents have found that modern "church kids" live and talk much like their secular peers. Christian Smith, a sociologist who has extensively studied the lives of religious young people, has found that in general, American teens practice what he calls "Moralistic Therapeutic Deism," a bland, relativistic spirituality that emphasizes doing good, feeling good, and believing in a benevolent, harmless, one-size-fits-all God. Smith's book *Soul Searching* includes many brief and often depressing interviews with teens conducted by the sociologist and his staff. For example, Smith comments:

> VIEWED IN TERMS of the absolute historical centrality of the Protestant conviction about salvation by God's grace alone, through faith alone and not by any human good works, many belief professions by Protestant teens, including numerous conservative Protestant teens, in effect discard that essential Protestant gospel. One 15–year–old white

conservative Protestant boy from Mississippi, for instance, explained, "If you just do the right thing and don't do any-thing bad, I mean nothing really bad, you know you'll go to heaven. If you don't, you're screwed [laughs], that's about it." Similarly, this 16–year–old black conservative Protestant girl from Pennsylvania told us, "Being a Christian, um, don't do many sins, read the Bible, go to church, living godly, that's about it. It's basically not committing sin, basically." (Smith, 136)

In another section, Smith discusses the absence of a connec-tion between biblical thinking and day-to-day life:

QUITE OFTEN, TEENS said they did not think their religious faith affected their family relationships, they did not believe religion was relevant to the conduct of a dating relation-ship, they did not see that religion affected their life at school, and so on. This was often even true for teens who in the religious discussion explicitly said that faith was important and influential in their lives. One 16–year–old white mainline Protestant girl from Michigan, for example, who explicitly stated, "Religion is very important to me," denied in every other section of the interview that religion had anything to do with her relationships, dating, school work, or any other aspect of her ordinary life. (Smith, 140)

One could cite numerous other examples from Smith's text that make this same point. At base, it is clear that many modern teens from a wide variety of churches have little sense of the personal importance and eternal significance of Christ and His Word.

The teenage years are known for their difficulty and turmoil, and that must be stated. In addition, Christian parents cannot produce faith in their children, and even the best parents may see their children drift away from the faith. But these necessary qualifications do not silence the point made above. On a broad level, Christians and churches are struggling to pass on biblical Christianity. Many of us are not living robustly Christian lives; a good portion of our children are not, either.

A Brief Sweep of Factors
Behind the Current Situation

It is not the purpose of this chapter to exhaustively trace the factors that led to our current situation. We are more concerned with the state of things on the ground, and cannot take the space necessary to sketch out a full-fledged answer to this important question, so the following survey will be brief. Readers desiring to look into this further would do well to look at a number of volumes cited in this chapter, including David Wells's texts *No Place for Truth, Above All Earthly Pow'rs,* and *The Courage to Be Protestant.*

To concisely identify a few key factors, we need to travel

back in time a couple of centuries to eighteenth-century Europe, the "Age of Lights" or "Enlightenment." In this era, a number of key thinkers reacted against state churches and their dogma, labeling religious faith "superstition" and emphasizing the primacy of the human intellect. They questioned the authority and truthfulness of the Bible and sought to strip it of elements they deemed false and superstitious. It took some time for this manner of thinking to trickle down into society, but eventually, many European countries once characterized by religious faith became increasingly secularized in the nineteenth and twentieth centuries. This unbelieving line of thought spread to churches and seminaries and caused many in traditional church traditions to fall away from orthodox faith.

In time, religious leaders began to doubt even their hardline liberal commitments. In the second half of the twentieth century, they accommodated to the secular "postmodern" spirit, avoiding "dogma" of any kind, and embracing mystery. Instead of emphasizing absolute truth, they spoke of truth for communities. That is, certain communities believed one way, and that was truth for them; others might believe something entirely different, and that was also true (for them). Some Christians from both conservative and liberal backgrounds adopted this spirit, creating a new kind of church, one light on doctrine and heavy on personal experience and mystery.

At the same time, the intellectual weakness of the church and the accommodation of its formative seminaries to liberal modes of thought drove many conservative Christian leaders to look to the booming American business sector for clues to vitality and growth. In the process, some American Christians lost connection to a Bible-centered model of preaching and, accordingly, a biblical worldview. Others who remained consciously biblical concentrated themselves so narrowly on political and social concerns that they seemed to make the church another Political Action Committee. Many "mainline" churches adopted liberal doctrines and deemphasized or even discarded fundamental doctrines of Christianity, though in the present day, a biblical witness of varying size persists in some denominations. Still more professing Christians have lost confidence and interest in local churches and have invested in parachurch organizations, trusting national leaders and ministries to lead them from afar without meaningful contact with a body of believers.

Pragmatism and Postmodernism in the Church

With the rise of the financial market and the cultural abandonment of various tenets of a Christian worldview, many of our evangelical churches have shifted from a richly biblical and theological perspective to one driven by pragmatic concerns. Congregations often do not make this shift to spite doctrine; instead, they do it because they think it will bring health and growth. Though they may mean well, a concern for numbers over a concern for personal faith makes it easy for nominalism to creep into the church. When churches concentrate so much on bringing people in, they can lose sight of building people up. That kind of atmosphere can make it easy for people to adopt a half-hearted faith, a Christianity that may be no Christianity at all.

Cultural critic Os Guinness has written persuasively about the pragmatic mindset in the church. He notes that

> THE CONCERN "WILL IT WORK?" has long overshadowed "Is it true?" Theology has given way to technique. Know–whom has faded before know–how. Serving God has subtly been deformed into servicing the self. At its worst, the result is a shift from faith to the "faith in faith," which—along with faith in religion—is a perniciously distinctive American heresy. But even at its best, pragmatism results in an evan–gelicalism rich in ingenuity and organization but poor in spirituality and superficial, if not banal, in doctrine. We have become the worldliest Christians in America. (Guinness, 59)

This is a key problem. As Guinness identifies, many of our churches have bought into the modern American consumer mindset in which we understand ourselves primarily as consumers and our churches as service-providers. Some pastors no longer preach prophetic, biblically robust, God-centered sermons meant to feed the people of God a delicious and healthy biblical "meal." Instead, they offer the church short, airy homilies aimed at the practical and psychological "needs" of people.

Because size is at a premium in modern church life, many

Christians wander through their church buildings, not knowing where to begin to connect with believers on a meaningful level. The result is, in some cases, churches with huge membership rolls but little biblical discipleship and corporate involvement (the same can be true of small churches as well). Few people have effectively studied what our modern church culture, with its emphasis on size and numbers, has done to discipleship. Where are the vital intergenerational connections spoken of in the Pastoral Epistles (Titus 2, for example)? Where is church discipline and its essential display of the church's commitment to holiness before the Lord (Matthew 18:20)? How do Christians in large churches without significant corporate togetherness care for one another in meaningful ways (Galatians 6:2)? These and many other biblically derived questions go unasked and unanswered in many Christian circles today.

Pragmatism, however, is not the only temptation that churches face today. As noted earlier, certain corners of evangelicalism have shifted away from staunch doctrinal stances. They have instead accommodated postmodernism and have moved from teaching the absolute truths of Scripture. They give great weight to personal experience and emphasize that as the world has changed, so the church and the church's gospel must change. They consider those who profess belief in absolute truth and morality to be "judgmental," the worst sin of all in a postmodern world. Leading progressive thinkers like Brian McLaren sound this horn, while figures like D. A. Carson, Kevin DeYoung, and Ted Kluck have countered this new way of thinking. The postmodern wing of the evangelical church is notoriously hard to pin down, but it presents a threat to the health of the church today, just as pragmatism does.

An Undeveloped Christian Mind

These trends have not had only macro-level effects. On the ground level, many Christians have an undeveloped Christian mind and a largely untouched life. The church, not the academy or any other institution, is responsible for the spiritual development of the people of God. David Wells drives to the root of this problem in his cultural analysis, arguing in a number of places that the modern church has imbibed the spirit of modern culture, which is intellectually fragmented, market-driven, style-based, personality-driven, and morally relativistic. He contends that:

> [C]ONSUMER SOCIETY PRODUCES only brief, fleeting connections and no bonding in the melting pot. The more descriptive image of the postmodern experience would be not the melting pot but the cocktail party. This is the place of brief encounter where those who may be strangers perform the ritual of instant, but evaporating community, one that springs into being as the sun sets and is gone before the moon arises. The modern self, as a result, has grown very thin, insubstantial, and distracted. It lives in a world of fleeting experiences and constantly shifting images, images

> which we create and by which we sometimes even pass
> ourselves off as something we are not. In this world of
> images and shadows, the only constant is not the self
> behind them, or the self consuming them, but the corpo-
> rations which create and exploit them. (*Above All Earthly
> Pow'rs*, 45)

Wells's elegant imagery does not obscure the heft of his
thought. In a consumerist world where advertising reigns and
ethical and spiritual ideas must kneel in the presence of the
almighty market, we have become "insubstantial" people with
"thin" selves. In other words, we are not deeply rooted in any
sense. Oftentimes, we don't think profoundly; we don't connect meaningfully; we don't focus extendedly. We can all too
easily flit through life, trying new experiences, inventing new
selves through online media. We watch endless amounts of
television, keep a constant vigil over our email accounts, and
update 800 of our closest friends when we make a piece of
toast, but we often cannot be bothered to read, or think, or
delve into the lives of unbelievers who are everywhere around
us. We have focused on ourselves, pumping ourselves up
through self-esteem exercises, redefining our sins as "ten-
dencies" that require therapy of one kind or another, and dis-
carding traditional marks of maturity to gratify desires we
refuse to tame. In the process, we have not grown. We have
shrunk.

God, it seems, has shrunk with us. So says Wells, noting
that in our society:

GOD IS MUCH FRIENDLIER, too. Gone are the notes of
judgment, though these are more displaced than denied,
and they are replaced by those of love and acceptance. . . .
Sin is preached but is presented more in terms of how it
"harms the individual, rather than how it offends a holy
God. Sin, in short, prevents us from realizing our full
potential." Conversion is insisted upon but then, paradoxi-
cally, it is the this-worldly benefits that are accentuated, the
practical benefits of knowing Christ receiving all the attention with scarcely a look at what happens if we turn away
from him. (*Above All Earthly Pow'rs*, 306)

Here is the ultimate mark of our decline. Because the church
has largely lost its theological orientation in the wake of the
Enlightenment and the ascendancy of a consumer culture,
we have, perhaps unwittingly, redefined our God and what it
means to know Him. He is a preference, a choice, who when we
convert bestows upon us what we've always deserved. With little
grip on a biblical understanding of the Almighty, we who are
called to be shaped in His holy image have done the reverse: we
have shaped Him in our image. As a result, He looks a lot like us.

The Untouched Lives of
Many Professing Christians

We have looked into the life and thought of the contemporary evangelical church in this brief little chapter. We have

found reasons for discouragement in numerous places—in the way evangelicals live, in the testimony given by their children, in the sway pragmatism and postmodernism hold in church life. The church, created by God to represent His holiness in this world, has instead accommodated the culture, adopting in many cases its practices, concerns, and even ideologies. In too many of our churches, Christians do not live or think differently from the world. Many may simply be struggling as all who follow Christ in a sinful world do. But the combined weight of this testimony should lead us to consider another possibility: a sizeable portion of Christians are nominal believers, people who profess faith in Christ but who do not truly know the Lord.

We know from Scripture that until Christ returns, the church will be imperfect. It will have some "wheat"—some true believers—and some "tares"—those who falsely profess faith (see Matthew 13). At the same time, we must also know that the church can grow strong or wax weak depending on its love for the Lord and His Word. In some eras, the church thrives; in others, it weakens. In our age, we need to identify the significant challenges and temptations before us in order that we might glorify God and thrive.

There are Christian movements, churches, and leaders that give us great hope. We should support these works of God and take much encouragement from them. Though we do believe that nominalism affects every church in some way, it does not affect all churches to the same extent. We would not desire for churches and Christians to embrace a posture of needless fear or anxiety. Many churches in this era are recognizing the importance of church membership and doctrinal discipleship. Where these biblical practices are celebrated and where, in general, the Word is faithfully preached and accountability and togetherness are pursued, we should expect to find health, and encouragement, and the sweet savor of God's glory.

But we must not be naïve. As we will see, Edwards's own example shows us that biblical preaching and zeal for the gospel cannot guarantee church health. We face even greater challenges in our day. It is clear that the culture is increasingly moving away from Christian belief. The academy, the media, and the entertainment world challenge Christian faith on intellectual, spiritual, and moral fronts. Pragmatism lures us with promises of vast size and huge budgets. Postmodernism suggests we lay down our absolute truth and morality. Everywhere we are urged to esteem ourselves and make God smaller, the greatest sin of all. Churches and Christians of all kinds are confronted by these problems. Sadly, many who give in on these fronts and suffer from weak faith and weak morality may not merely struggle in their faith. They may have none at all.

We do not have an easy road before us, as Israel's history and the church's past teach us. In the next chapter, we will find abundant proof that even a theological titan like Jonathan Edwards, living in a time and place amenable to biblical Christianity, struggled mightily to counter nominal faith. As we learn from his heroic example in successive chapters, we will discover how we can respond to our present situation and stand for true Christianity in this fallen world.

 Embracing True Christianity

The Need for Evangelical Self-Examination in Our Denominations and Churches

*T*he problem of nominalism described above requires that we adopt a spirit of humility and self-examination before the Lord. Church history abundantly testifies to the idea that nominalism is a problem that all churches and denominations face. Some circumstances may expedite the spread of these problems, and others may more effectively fight them, but all Christians and churches would do well to put down pride and address this challenge with sobriety and confidence in a sovereign God. We cannot take refuge in membership rolls, especially when in seemingly booming denominations, experts suggest that perhaps half of the many millions of members on church rolls rarely set foot in a church building, let alone exercise vibrant faith.

Beyond our denominations, we cannot look around our churches and assume that attendees know the Lord because they belong to the church or attend it faithfully. To put this more simply, just because someone raises their hand in a time of singing doesn't mean that they are a Christian. Just because someone smiles when greeted, gives generously to the church, and signs up to help in various programs does not mean that they are a Christian. Just because someone has said they are a Christian does not mean that they are. All of the above may sound tough, but we must confront hard realities in a time of great challenge for the church.

We need to be very careful about thinking that a Christian necessarily looks and acts a certain way. We must constantly keep in mind that however healthy our particular congregation, there is no church, no style of worship, no creed one recites that can in itself ensure the conversion of a sinner. Recognizing this fact alone can help us begin to examine our churches and denominations.

The Need for Sober Evangelical Self-Examination in Our Families

*O*ne of the scariest things about the data presented above is the sad state of the spiritual lives of many children who have grown up in sound churches. The inability of many children from Christian families to articulate even the simplest biblical truths—who God is and what saving faith is, for starters—shows that many of us have fallen short in our efforts to instill a biblical way of thinking and living in our children. We cannot, of course, save our children by our efforts, but the Bible makes very clear that parental training greatly affects the spiritual lives of our offspring (Proverbs 22:6).

Contrary to our event-centered, leader-oriented, excitement-driven view of childhood training, the Bible seems to suggest that children learn best about true faith in the simple, mundane things of life, in watching parents honor God in the midst of the normal rhythms of everyday life (Deuteronomy 6:7). Though parents may feel inadequate to teach and train, they can take great comfort in knowing that an authentic witness, coupled by sound instruction, has great power. The lives of countless believers raised by godly parents testify to this reality. Though they may buttress our parenting, we do not *need* flashy children's programs or charismatic youth speakers. We need to be godly parents whose lives back up our faith.

CHAPTER TWO

The Problem of Nominal Christianity in Edwards's Day

IN THE FORMER PART of this great work of God amongst us, till it got to its height, we seemed to be wonderfully smiled upon and blessed in all respects. Satan (as has been already observed) seemed to be unusually restrained: persons that before had been involved in melancholy, seemed to be as it were waked up out of it; and those that had been entangled with extraordinary temptations, seemed wonderfully to be set at liberty; and not only so, but it was the most remarkable time of health, that ever I knew since I have been in the town. (*Works* 4, 205)

*T*his was Jonathan Edwards's assessment of his town's spiritual health in 1735. Just a little while after this happy state, however, a period of decline and despair struck the community. "In the latter part of May," Edwards wrote, "it began to be very sensible that the Spirit of God was gradually withdrawing from us, and after this time Satan seemed to be more let loose, and raged in a dreadful manner" (*Works* 4, 206). The great promise of the 1735 revival waned as the town gradually settled into a spiritual malaise.

This was not an uncommon experience for the Northampton pastor. As his career unfolded, Edwards confronted the specter of a lukewarm spirituality on numerous occasions. In fact, it is not too much to say that this was the primary burden of Edwards's pastoral ministry. Laboring in an age when all townspeople supported the minister through taxation and attended church services upon penalty of law, Edwards preached to a people that in large number often showed little interest in the things of God. Never one to take a challenge lying down, Edwards devoted continual energy to fighting this problem, urging his congregation in sermon after sermon to take their sin seriously and to embrace the gift of Christ's grace.

His example instructs us today as we wrestle with our own modern versions of tepid spirituality. He devoted considerable attention to unmasking nominal faith by exposing its weaknesses and revealing its inconsistencies. He never let himself grow satisfied with high attendance and easy praise. He could not rest until the people under his watch understood the gravity of their situation and came to grapple with their spiritual condition. The knowledge that he would give an account to the Lord on the last day for his shepherding of his people rested heavily on his soul, driving him to attack lukewarm faith in pursuit of true Christianity.

In this chapter, we will look primarily at Edwards's analysis of the lukewarm Christian. We will look at a sermon entitled "Living Unconverted Under Eminent Means of Grace," move to a substantial selection from the *Faithful Narrative of the Surprising Work of God*, and then examine sermons entitled "Many Mansions" and "True Grace Distinguished from the Experience of Devils." Through this analysis, we will gain wisdom into how Edwards thought about the problem of nominalism and how he addressed it. We'll see that the initial step in fighting nominalism is to identify and critique it. So begins our response to a problem that only God can ultimately conquer.

"Living Unconverted" Under a Godly Minister

Edwards knew the face of nominal Christianity well. He grew up in a pastor's home and possessed keen abilities of discernment from an early age. He was not fooled by cultural Christianity, different as it would have looked in his day, when most New England residents attended church and would have assented to the basic doctrines of the faith. Though one might think this kind of setting ideal to the spread of true faith, Edwards was painfully aware of the lack of vibrant Christian living among the Northampton residents, a point he made abundantly clear in the very first sermon he preached as pastor in 1729. Memorializing his recently deceased grandfather, Solomon Stoddard, Edwards rebuked many of his parishioners in "Living Unconverted Under Eminent Means of Grace," a sermon based on Jeremiah 6:29–30. The people of Northampton had benefited immensely from Stoddard's ministry, Edwards pointed out, though their lives displayed far less of the benefits than they should have:

> THERE HAVE [BEEN] FEW PLACES that have enjoyed such eminent powerful means of grace as you of this place have enjoyed. You have lived all your days under a most clear, convincing dispensation of God's word. The whole land is full of gospel light, but this place has been distinguishingly blessed of God with excellent means for a long time under your now deceased minister.

Edwards then turned up the heat, making his subject matter personal:

> AND IT ARGUES a dismal degree of obduracy and blindness, that persons could stand it out under such a ministry. In what a clear and awakening manner have you hundreds of times had your danger and misery in a natural condition set before you! How clearly have you had the way of sal-

vation shown to you, and how movingly have you had the encouragements of the gospel offered to you!

Such as can live all their days under such means of awakening and of conversion, and have stood it out and have been proof against such preaching, are undoubtedly of exceeding hard hearts. They that are still unawakened, doubtless their hearts are much harder than if they had not lived under such great advantages. Powerful preaching, if it don't awaken, it hardens more than other preaching.

The pastor concluded the point with a vivid warning:

THOSE MEANS ARE NOW GONE; you'll have them no more. You have stood it out until the bellows are burnt. You had the preaching, the calls and warnings of your eminent deceased minister till he was worn out in calling and warning and exhorting of you. God was so gracious, and so loathe that you should perish, that he continued his ability of preaching to wonderment. But the founder melted in vain as to you. He did not cease blowing till the bellows were worn out, as it were burnt out, in vain, trying if he could not extract some true silver from amongst the lead. He was very loathe to give you over till he had persuaded, and God seemed loathe to give you over by continuing of him so long to call upon you and warn you. But how many wicked are there that are not yet plucked away? (Works 14, 367–69)

Edwards sought to awaken his spiritually sleeping hearers by reminding them of the great advantage they had long enjoyed in sitting under a faithful preacher like Stoddard. Not many people "have enjoyed such eminent powerful means of grace as you," challenged a young Edwards. What had this forceful preaching met with? Among other things, declared Edwards, "a dismal degree of obduracy and blindness" such that Stoddard preached "till he was worn out in calling and warning and exhorting of you." Edwards could not have been more direct. If the lukewarm of Northampton did not soon repent of their half-hearted Christianity, they would lose all opportunity to repent, and the gospel they respected but never fully embraced would disappear from view.

The lukewarm members of Edwards's congregation made a common mistake. They committed themselves to the trappings of religion: respectable decorum, nice clothes, a pleasant churchly demeanor, and a quiet communal life. They would not, however, curb their appetites, mortify their secret sins, invest themselves in gospel work, and serve the church with their whole heart. Many of them undoubtedly took pride in the communal eminence of Stoddard, enjoying their association with such an important pastor in an age when pastors ruled their communities, but it seems that they ultimately failed to look beyond Stoddard's status to consider the import of his message.

The Pastor's Personal Experience
with Spiritual Decline

The problem of nominalism in Stoddard's day persisted in Edwards's own. His initial sermon shows that he was committed to fighting this scourge of the church. In the midst of this difficult work in the mid-1730s, he witnessed one of the more bountiful seasons of his ministry. Through the faithful preaching of the Word and a few key events, including the conversion of an influential young woman, a revival broke out in Northampton and surrounding towns, sweeping many into the church. It was a joyous time.

The fruits of revival soon gave way to a wave of doubt and apathy in Northampton. The pastor believed that the devil was urging some who had come under conviction to commit suicide. As noted in his revival report *A Faithful Narrative of the Surprising Work of God*, published in 1737, one Northampton man who had long struggled with depression did take his life. Following this:

> MULTITUDES IN THIS and other towns seemed to have it strongly suggested to 'em, and pressed upon 'em, to do as this person had done. And many that seemed to be under no melancholy, some pious persons that had no special darkness, or doubts about the goodness of their state, nor were under any special trouble or concern of mind about anything spiritual or temporal, yet had it urged upon 'em,

as if somebody had spoke to 'em, "Cut your own throat, now is good opportunity: *now, NOW!*" So that they were obliged to fight with all their might to resist it, and yet no reason suggested to 'em why they should do it.

Following these scary occurrences, the fires of revival died out, according to Edwards:

AFTER THESE THINGS the instances of conversion were rare here in comparison of what they had before been. . . . But religion remained here, and I believe in some other places, the main subject of conversation for several months after this. And there were some turns, wherein God's work seemed something to revive, and we were ready to hope that all was going to be renewed again: yet in the main there was a gradual decline of that general, engaged, lively spirit in religion, which had been before.

The pastor went on to express encouragement about the effects of the revival, though he noted ominously that some of them might fade with time:

I CAN'T SAY THAT there has been no instance of any one person that has carried himself so that others should justly be stumbled concerning his profession; nor am I so vain as to imagine that we han't been mistaken concerning any that we have entertained a good opinion of, or that there

> are none that pass amongst us for sheep, that are indeed
> wolves in sheep's clothing; who probably may some time
> or other discover themselves by their fruits. (*Works* 4, 206–9)

Edwards's foresight proved true. Though many people who came to faith in the revival prospered spiritually, others fell away, leaving Edwards to battle discouragement and doubts about his own pastoral ability and faithfulness.

This section from the *Faithful Narrative* helps us to understand Edwards and his day better, for it encapsulates one of the pastor's recurring experiences throughout his ministry. Indeed, this was not the only time in his career that the Northampton pastor watched as the joy of spiritual awakening gave way to discouragement and malaise. Even in the happiest moments of his career, it seems, Edwards often had to confront religious declension.

Seeking Earthly Mansions
Over Heavenly Mansions

Edwards sometimes grew openly frustrated with the spiritual lukewarmness that he saw in his people. We glimpse a bit of his frustration in a sermon called "Many Mansions" based on John 14:2 and delivered in 1737 after his church, by the instigation of the town leadership, began reordering the pew seating system on the basis of familial wealth. Formerly, the church had ordered its pews according to communal reputation, based on age and "civic usefulness." The new system, structured along financial concerns, infuriated Edwards. In his sermon preached just after the new system took hold, Edwards warned his people of the consequences of this decision:

> TAKE WARNING BY THESE warnings of providence to improve your time, that you may have a mansion in heaven. We have a house of worship newly erected amongst us, which now you have a seat in, and probably are pleased with the ornaments of it; and though you have a place among others in so comely an house, you know not how little a while you shall have a place in this house of God. Here are a couple snatched away by death that had met in it but a few times, that have been snatched out of it before it was fully finished, and never will have any more a seat in it. You know not how soon you may follow. And then of great importance will it be to you to have a seat in God's house above.

Edwards then devoted attention to the young people of his congregation, who in his eyes were apt to esteem worldly things like social rank:

> LET OUR YOUNG PEOPLE therefore take warning from hence, and don't [act] such fools as to neglect seeking a place and mansion in heaven. Young persons are especially apt to be taken with the pleasing things of this world. You

are now, it may be, much pleased with hopes of your future
circumstances in this world, much pleased with the ornaments of that house of worship that you with others have
a place in. But, alas, do you not too little consider how soon
you may be taken away from all these things, and no more
forever have any part in any mansion, or house, or enjoyment, or business under the sun. Therefore let it be your
main care to secure an everlasting habitation for hereafter.
(*Works* 19, 743–44)

The pastor concluded by exhorting congregants nursing their
wounds over their newfound seating location to take sight of
another realm, where this foolish decision would not matter
in the least:

AND IF THERE BE any that ben't seated in their seats,
because they are too low for 'em, let them consider that it
is but a very little while before it will [be] all one to you,
whether you have sat high or low here. But it will be of
infinite and everlasting concern to you, where your seat is
in another world. Let your great concern be while in this
world, so to improve your opportunity in God's house in
that world, whether you sit high or low, as that you may
have [a] glorious and distinguished mansion in God's house
in heaven, where you may be fixed in your place in that
eternal assembly in everlasting rest. Let the main thing that

you prize in God's house be not the outward ornaments of
it, [or] an high seat in it, but the word of Christ, and God's
ordinance in it. And spend your time here in seeking Christ,
that he may prepare a place for you in his Father's house;
that so when he comes again to this world, he may take
you to him; that where he is, there you may be also. (*Works*
19, 746)

In retrospect, the whole affair seems rather silly and surprising given the unique position of the Northampton church.
Here was a people given a rich pulpit ministry by the Lord
and considerable financial ability to promote the work of the
kingdom, and yet they fought and fussed over the ideal location of their posteriors. In such a climate, Edwards pushed
his people to serve the church, not use it for social climbing
and status-building: "Let the main thing that you prize in
God's house be not the outward ornaments of it, [or] an high
seat in it, but the word of Christ, and God's ordinance in it."

As the pastor saw it, the professing Christian with lukewarm faith seeks the outward things of religion and asks the
church to serve them. The true Christian, however, takes joy
not most in what the church does for them, but in what God
is doing in and through the church. Many in Edwards's own
church had the latter mindset, unfortunately, a reality that
reveals that Edwards had to fight nominalism on a considerable scale even in his day. Neither a state church nor a godly
pastor could ensure that church members knew the Lord. As

is often the case, many were too busy making much of themselves to make much of the Savior, the Lord Jesus Christ.

The Shape and Nature of True Grace

Edwards did not content himself with exposing the behaviors that marked a nominal Christian. He also worked hard to uncover the specious beliefs of worldly church members and labored to strip away pretenses of belief with careful arguments and biblical reasoning. In a notable sermon preached in 1752 on James 2:19, "True Grace Distinguished from the Experience of Devils," he showed that even devils had knowledge of spiritual things and experienced emotions resulting from spiritual realities. Believers who grounded their faith in mere biblical knowledge, and in the simple experience of various emotions related to their professed faith, had no more cause to assure themselves of their conversion than did the most wicked devil of Satan's realm.

Edwards first discussed in "True Grace" how head knowledge—he called it "speculative knowledge"—of biblical doctrines does not signal the presence of saving faith. Satan himself possesses such knowledge, said the pastor:

> WE MAY HENCE INFER, that no degree of speculative knowledge of things of religion, is any certain sign of saving grace. The devil, before his fall, was among those bright and glorious angels of heaven, which are represented as morning stars, and flames of fire, that excel in strength

and wisdom. And though he be now become sinful, yet his
sin has not abolished the faculties of the angelic nature; as
when man fell, he did not lose the faculties of the human
nature. (*Works* 25, 613)

Edwards offered the following gripping words as a summation
of this teaching: "The devil is orthodox in his faith; he believes
the true scheme of doctrine; he is no Deist, Socinian, Arian,
Pelagian, or Antinomian; the articles of his faith are all sound,
and what he is thoroughly established in" (*Works* 25, 617).
Indeed, one could know any number of hefty theological concepts, as Satan does, and still not possess saving faith:

> THEREFORE IT IS MANIFEST, from my text and doctrine,
> that no degree of speculative knowledge of things of reli-
> gion, is any certain sign of true piety. Whatever clear notions
> a man may have of the attributes of God, and doctrine of
> the trinity; the nature of the two covenants, the economy of
> the persons of the trinity, and the part which each person
> has in the affair of man's redemption; if he can discourse
> never so excellently of the offices of Christ, and the way of
> salvation by him, and the admirable methods of divine
> wisdom; and the harmony of the various attributes of God
> in that way; if he can talk never so clearly and exactly of
> the method of the justification of a sinner, and of the nature
> of conversion, and the operations of the Spirit of God, in

> applying the redemption of Christ; giving good distinctions,
> happily solving difficulties, and answering objections; in a
> manner tending greatly to the enlightening the ignorant,
> to the edification of the church of God, and the conviction
> of gainsayers; and the great increase of light in the world:
> if he has more knowledge of this sort than hundreds of true
> saints, of an ordinary education, and most divines; yet all
> is no certain evidence of any degree of saving grace in the
> heart. (*Works* 25, 616)

Though we may possess theological knowledge and even a
strong drive to know the Word, Edwards calls us to check our
hearts and the hearts of our fellow church members. Is doctrine merely fodder for debate? Do we simply store up biblical concepts like impersonal data? Edwards prompts us to ask
these questions in order that we might avoid a faith consist-
ing only of believed but impersonal truths.

The Northampton pastor also challenged emotive faith,
teaching that no emotional state, however strongly felt, could
guarantee that a sinner possessed saving faith. Fear of judgment, for example, might well result from a real understanding of divine wrath, but without any interior response of faith:

> THERE ARE MANY TERRORS, that some persons, who are
> concerned for their salvation, are the subjects of, which are
> not from any proper awakenings of conscience, or apprehen-
> sions of truth; but from melancholy, or frightful impressions

on their imagination; or some groundless apprehensions, and the delusions, and false suggestions of Satan. But if they have had never so great, and long-continued terrors, from real awakenings, and convictions of truth, and views of things as they are; this is no more than what is in the devils, and will be in all wicked men, in another world. However stupid and senseless most ungodly men are now, all will be effectually awakened at last: there will [be] no such thing as slumbering in hell. (*Works* 25, 618)

Edwards's sketch of the terrors of judgment demonstrated that fearing God's wrath did not mark a person as a true believer. But neither did a desire to be free of that judgment prove the existence of saving faith in the heart:

THE DEVILS, DOUBTLESS, long for deliverance from the misery they suffer, and from that greater misery which they expect. If they tremble through fear of it, they must, necessarily, earnestly desire to be delivered from it. Wicked men, are in Scripture, represented as longing for the privileges of the righteous, when the door is shut, and they are shut out from among them: they come to the door, and cry, "Lord, Lord, open to us." Therefore, we are not to look on all desires, or all desires that are very earnest and vehement, as certain evidences of a pious heart. There are earnest desires of a religious nature, which the saints have, that are

> the proper breathings of a new nature, and distinguishing qualities of true saints: but there are also longings, which unregenerate men may have, which are often mistaken for marks of godliness: they think they hunger and thirst after righteousness; and have earnest desires after God and Christ, and long for heaven; when indeed, all is to be resolved into desires of salvation, from self-love; and so is a longing which arises from no higher principles, than the earnest desires of devils. (*Works* 25, 624–25)

One can fear God and His judgment with the full extent of one's being and still not know the Lord, according to Edwards. Mere recognition of God's existence and His hatred for sin and willingness to punish it does not in any way justify or save the sinner. This, after all, is the conviction of devils. They "long for deliverance from the misery they suffer" (see Mark 5:1–13, for example). They are, of course, unconverted, but they live in abject fear of God's punishment of sin, as do so many people who will not, for whatever reason, repent of their sinful ways.

On the other hand, a vague pleasure in the things of religion, however orthodox, did not necessarily signal a converted heart, either. In the section below, Edwards discusses how an unregenerate sinner could, acting out of a natural love for oneself, find happiness in religion and religious causes. In fact, even a devil, Edwards asserted, could act in this way:

IF YOUR LOVE TO GOD, has its first source from nothing else than a supposed immediate divine witness, or any other supposed evidence, that Christ died for you in particular, and that God loves you; it springs from no higher principles than self-love; which is a principle that reigns in the hearts of devils. Self-love is sufficient, without grace, to cause men to love those that love them, or that they imagine love them, and make much of them; Luke 6:32, "For if ye love them which love you, what thank have you? For sinners also love those that love them." And would not the hearts of devils be filled with great joy, if they, by any means, should take up a confident persuasion that God had pardoned them, and was become their friend, and that they should be delivered from that wrath which they now are in trembling expectation of. If the devils go so far as you have heard, even in their circumstances, being totally cast off, and given up to unrestrained wickedness, being without hope, knowing that God is, and ever will be their enemy, they suffering his wrath without mercy: how far may we reasonably suppose they might go, in imitation of grace and pious experience, if they had the same degree of knowledge, as clear views, and as strong conviction, under circumstances of hope, and offers of mercy; and being the subjects of common grace, restraining their corruptions, and assisting and exciting the natural principles of reason, conscience, etc.? (*Works* 25, 632)

Having established his point that devils could, given a certain set of circumstances, exercise a certain brand of religiously oriented behavior, Edwards then listed the natural convictions devils might hold, all of which line up with orthodox Christian theology and experience:

SUCH GREAT CONVICTION of conscience; such a sense of the importance of eternal things; such affecting views of the awful majesty, greatness, power, holiness, justice, and truth of God, and such a sense of his great grace to the saints, if they, or anything like 'em, should be in the heart of a sinner, in this world; at the same time that he, from some strong impression on his imagination, of Christ appearing to him, or sweet words spoken to him, or by some other means, has suddenly, after great terrors, imbibed a strong confidence, that now, this great God, is his friend and father, has released him from all the misery he feared, and has promised him eternal happiness: I say, such things would, doubtless, vastly heighten his ecstasy of joy, and raise the exercise of natural gratitude (that principle from whence sinners love those that love them), and would occasion a great imitation of many graces, in strong exercises. Is it any wonder then, that multitudes under such a sort of affection, are deceived? (*Works* 25, 632–33)

In this passage, Edwards stretches the bounds of what a devil might actually believe theologically, though his point is abundantly clear: a person living under the influence of common grace (as we all do) and acting out of some form of self-love (as we all do) could easily take pleasure in the doctrines and experience of Christianity without actually knowing the Lord in a salvific sense. The truths of Christianity can appear beautiful on a surface level to the unconverted heart. They may elicit emotion and thus affect a person's outward demeanor, just as a child's smile, or a strong ethical conviction, or the promise of hope in a distressing situation may do the same without converting the heart. A person may out of a knowledge of biblical doctrine live a happy and hopeful life, trusting in God's providence, living gratefully in some sense for Christ's sacrifice. However, unless this knowledge is personally applied in repentance of sin and wholehearted faith in the person and work of Jesus Christ, it does not save us from sin and judgment (see James 2:18–26).

Confronting Nominal Christianity

As this chapter has shown, Jonathan Edwards sought to wake lax professors up and to show them that though they considered themselves truly saved for one reason or another, they stood on far shakier ground than they might have thought. His experience, painful as it often was, taught him that nothing could prevent widespread nominalism—not a theocentric church, not a devout pastor-shepherd, not even biblically fueled revival. Sanctioned by Satan, the nominal Christian possessed all too many resources to deceive themselves about their true spiritual state, whether biblical knowledge, fear of judgment, religiously minded happiness, or other things. It is likely that these are the kinds of attributes many of the nominal Christians in our churches possess. They fear the Lord, and go to church, and do religious things, believing on some level that their involvement procures forgiveness and salvation.

In their encounter with true Christianity, these people taste something of the sweetness of religious devotion and biblical truth, though they do no more than sample these good things. They are not so convicted by judgment as to repent of their sin, and they are not so gripped by the glory of divine grace that they embrace Christ. They may know biblical doctrine, even to the point of being able to make a case for a certain scriptural teaching, but this truth has not transformed them. What needs to bore into the heart sits lightly on the conscience, skimming the surface but never penetrating to the soul.

Moving from Edwards's era to ours, the nominal Christian is something like a movie watcher who observes the story of Christianity as it plays out in the lives of true Christians. He comprehends the plot, shrinks back at the scary parts, and grows happy when the good guys win, but he never enters in. He pauses the story when he likes, fast forwards the parts he doesn't enjoy, and watches the scenes he prefers over and over again, shaping his perception of the story by his own preferences.

Then, when he sees fit, he stops it altogether. Through it all, he is unaware that just as the story fails to claim him, he is himself unclaimed by the story. He is a mere witness to a transforming reality that will soon pass him by.

Embracing True Christianity

Find Comfort in Edwards's Experience

Though our present situation discourages us in many ways, we can take some comfort in the fact that a pastor like Jonathan Edwards struggled just like we do. Deep piety, hefty preaching, and a brilliant mind cannot in themselves guarantee that a church will grow spiritually (or numerically), just as a CEO mentality, personal charm, and quick wit offer us no assurance of "success." Even if we work very hard to bring revival to the lost and spur on biblical zeal, we have no guaranteed positive response. In fact, even if our pastors faithfully preach the Bible and faithfully minister to their people, they may well face nominalism as Edwards did. Though we should take pains in our churches and homes to identify false faith and advance the truth, we must know that the Lord in His mysterious providence may or may not reward our work with lasting change and true revival.

Challenge People to Leave the Trappings of Religion

A central struggle in Edwards's fight against lukewarm Christianity was the love exhibited by many in his church for the trappings, but not the substance, of religion. Though the circumstances have changed, the issue remains. This is especially true in a day when many American Christians have witnessed unprecedented evangelical influence in many areas of cultural life—politics, entertainment, literature, social institutions, and more. This kind of "success" can create a culture in which people bask in the glow of Christianity without actually coming into contact with the true Light.

Without lapsing into hostile wariness about all of our activities, we need to look out for signs in our individual and church lives that show that we enjoy the trappings of the faith more than its substance. In Edwards's day, many people took more pride in their position in the pew than in their faith in Christ. The same can happen today. We can revel in our lush surroundings, and bask in the attention of fellow members, and spend all kinds of time and attention on our own concerns, forgetting the kingdom cause before us. This is what happened in Northampton—people became more focused on themselves than on the mission of the gospel. The same can happen to us today if we are not careful.

Find No Comfort in Knowledge, Emotion, or Impressions Alone

*A*s Edwards memorably showed, we cannot find confidence in spiritual knowledge, emotions, or impressions by themselves. Even a devil can theoretically possess any one of these things and be as far from grace and God as can be. We should of course encourage the development of biblical and theological knowledge, scripturally guided affections, and spiritual impressions and views based on the Bible. But these things in themselves cannot save a person and thus cannot assure a person. As we will see in the chapter to come, only the Lord's converting work can do this.

Different people will land in different categories here. Some will credit their faith to knowledge, others to feelings, others to impressions or views. When we hear such testimony, we need to push deeper, examining whether faith does exist in this one who claims Christ, or whether the experience of faith goes no deeper than simple knowledge of the truth, emotion of the heart, or vague senses of the intuition.

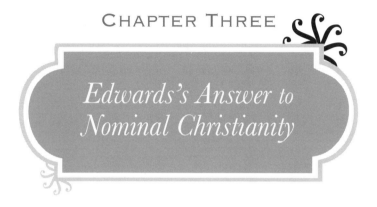

CHAPTER THREE

Edwards's Answer to Nominal Christianity

*O*ut with certainty, in with mystery. One of the key philo-sophical trends of the last century has been the shift from certainty to skepticism. Many thinkers, reacting against the intellectual arrogance of philosophers who emphasize the ability of the human mind to know things exhaustively, have emphasized paradox and mystery. People today still talk about "truth" and other foundational principles of life, but they do so in chastened language that communicates a lack of ulti-mate assurance about their subject. "Well, yeah, I think that's true, but it's true for me—I'm not trying to judge anyone or anything like that."

Many Christians have adopted aspects of this way of

thinking. "Well, yeah, I'm a Christian, and I believe in the gospel, but that's just my personal opinion." Aware that the current age does not look kindly on certainty, many Christians publicly downplay the intensity of their belief in God. They talk and think about their faith as more of a personal choice than a divine call. This shift in mind often affects the heart. "Yeah, I'm a Christian, but I don't necessarily believe in all the religious aspects of Christianity. I don't think that it's necessary to go to church. I'm more into spirituality than religion." In the wake of such muddled testimony, many people today have no clue what a true Christian is. As we saw in chapter 1, America is awash in nominalism. Many people claim to be Christian, even describing themselves as "born-again." But a very small percentage of that same group exhibits intentional religious commitment. In such a culture, confusion builds up about the nature of Christianity like rushing water against a dam.

Mired as we are in such a setting, we turn again to our theological guide, the Bible preacher Jonathan Edwards, who lived and worked in an era riddled with nominalism and spiritual compromise. Taking his cues from Holy Scripture, Edwards carved out a clear and compelling image of the authentic Christian life designed to bring his hearers and readers into saving contact with the biblical gospel. The pastor sketched out a portrait of the Christian faith that rendered it arresting and memorable, worth attention hundreds of years later.

In the last chapter, we looked at what Edwards said was *not* Christianity. In this chapter, we look at what Edwards believed was true Christianity. We have looked at the negative;

now we look at the positive side of true Christianity, observing its traits and key characteristics. In doing so, we look at a
section from "The Reality of Conversion," another from *Freedom of the Will*, excerpts from "Justification by Faith Alone"
and "A Divine and Supernatural Light," and several passages
from *Distinguishing Marks of a True Work of the Spirit of God*
and *Treatise on the Religious Affections.* In sum, we see that
while Edwards took pains to establish what true Christianity
was not (as seen in chapter 2), he also took special care to
sketch out an exciting portrait of true Christianity that will,
now as then, help us to recover a richly biblical understanding of conversion and the change it affects.

Conversion Is Real

The starting point for a discussion of Edwards's view of
conversion has to be this: he believed in it. He believed in the
quickening work of the Holy Spirit and its visible, effect. Over
against those who argued that Christian conversion was a myth,
a fairy tale, Edwards amassed numerous arguments for its
authenticity in his sermon "The Reality of Conversion," based
on John 3:10–11. There, he advanced the central claim that:

> THERE IS NO KIND of love in the world that has had such
> great, visible effects in men as love to Christ has had,
> though he be an unseen object, which [is] an evidence of a
> divine work in the hearts of men, infusing that love into
> them. Thus the voice of reason, Scripture and experience,

and the testimony of the best of men do all concur in it,
that there must be such a thing as conversion. (Kimnach, 89)

In the midst of nominal believers whose actions caused many
to doubt the realness of Christianity, Edwards made a bold
declaration: conversion is real. It is not a psychological eccen-
tricity; it is not an invention of religious types who want to
control others. Salvation, Edwards said, proceeds as a "divine
work." Salvation happens.

The Harmony of Mind and Will

The second step in a proper understanding of Edwards's
view of authentic conversion relates to his view of the human
will. Though a highly technical discussion, this matter boils
down to a basic principle that informs our understanding of
how a sinner comes to embrace the truth of the gospel. Some
in Edwards's day separated the decision of the mind from the
act of the will, arguing that the will did not necessarily follow
the "dictates" of the mind. Edwards refuted this argument at
length in his *Freedom of the Will*:

THINGS THAT EXIST in the view of the mind, have their
strength, tendency or advantage to move or excite its will,
from many things appertaining to the nature and circumstances of the thing viewed, the nature and circumstances
of the mind that views, and the degree and manner of its

view; which it would perhaps be hard to make a perfect enumeration of. But so much I think may be determined in general, without room for controversy, that whatever is perceived or apprehended by an intelligent and voluntary agent, which has the nature and influence of a motive to volition or choice, is considered or viewed as good; nor has it any tendency to invite or engage the election of the soul in any further degree than it appears such. For to say otherwise, would be to say, that things that appear have a tendency by the appearance they make, to engage the mind to elect them, some other way than by their appearing eligible to it; which is absurd. And therefore it must be true, in some sense, that the will always is as the greatest apparent good is. (*Works* 1, 142)

This quotation, though weighty, shows how closely the mind and heart are linked, and how essential it is that one fill one's mind with truth. What our mind fixates on will in turn "move or excite" our wills. In simpler terms, what we see as desirable, as pleasurable, as best, we will want.

This simple but important point clarifies conversion. We do not haphazardly come to faith, choosing to believe the gospel without intellectual assent. We believe in the gospel because we consider its claims in our minds, judge them to be right and good and beautiful, and then decide to give them our assent.

Conversion, then, involves the full measure of our minds, as does our subsequent transformation (Romans 12:1–2).

The Influence of The Holy Spirit

The Holy Spirit accomplished this work, which is a third prong of an Edwardsean understanding of conversion. As covered in *Jonathan Edwards on the Good Life*, Edwards believed that Adam and Eve fell away from God. When they did so, God removed the Spirit, the gift of His grace known as the "superior" or "spiritual" principles, from the human heart. Adam and Eve then followed their "natural" principles, their bodily appetites and desires, and disobeyed God, cursing the human race to be ruled by their natural and "inferior" principles by birth.

All of this changed, however, when the Holy Spirit moved in a human heart. The Spirit excited repentance in the sinner and became a "spring of new nature," as the pastor put it in his classic treatise *The Religious Affections*:

> THE SPIRIT OF GOD is given to the true saints to dwell in them, as his proper lasting abode; and to influence their hearts, as a principle of new nature, or as a divine supernatural spring of life and action. The Scriptures represent the Holy Spirit, not only as moving, and occasionally influencing the saints, but as dwelling in them as his temple, his proper abode, and everlasting dwelling place (1 Corinthians

3:16; 2 Corinthians 6:16; John 14:16–17). And he is represented as being there so united to the faculties of the soul,
that he becomes there a principle or spring of new nature
and life. (*Works* 2, 200)

The Holy Spirit caused the human heart to flare with life as
the spiritual principles, the superior graces and gifts of God,
took hold:

FROM THESE THINGS it is evident, that those gracious
influences which the saints are subjects of, and the effects
of God's Spirit which they experience, are entirely above
nature, altogether of a different kind from anything that
men find within themselves by nature, or only in the exercise of natural principles; and are things which no improve-
ment of those qualifications, or principles that are natural,
no advancing or exalting them to higher degrees, and no
kind of composition of them, will ever bring men to;
because they not only differ from what is natural, and from
everything that natural men experience, in degree and circumstances; but also in kind; and are of a nature vastly
more excellent. And this is what I mean by supernatural,
when I say, that gracious affections are from those influences that are supernatural. (*Works* 2, 205)

Possessing the Holy Spirit, Edwards noted, made a person "spiritual." The Holy Spirit made all the difference. He convinced the sinner's mind of the truthfulness of God, His Word, and His gospel message. In doing so, He regenerated the wicked heart and came to dwell spiritually in the new convert. He does not flit in and out of our hearts like a drifting traveler, roaming here and there. He lives in the believer, taking residence in the heart, giving us "gracious affections" that are "vastly more excellent" than our natural affections.

Edwards's vivid descriptions of the Spirit's work remind us that conversion, though involving our deepest mental processes, is driven by a person. By the Spirit's work, we find faith in a personal, triune God. We are thus converted not by an abstract theological principle, but by a living, active person.

The Vivifying Convictions of the Redeemed Heart

If we accept that our wills follow our minds, and that the Spirit saves our souls, how are we to understand the actual faith that God implants within us? Exactly what separates the converting work of God's Spirit from ordinary religious devotion? In his sermon "Justification by Faith Alone," Edwards gave a summation of the gospel that separates it from all other messages and schemes that ground salvation in human effort. Conversion happens the instant a person truly repents of their sin and puts their faith in the atoning death and life-giving resurrection of Jesus Christ:

WHEN CHRIST HAD ONCE undertaken with God, to stand for us, and put himself under our law, by that law he was obliged to suffer, and by the same law he was obliged to obey: by the same law, after he had taken man's guilt upon him, he himself being our surety, could not be acquitted, till he had suffered, nor rewarded till he had obeyed: but he was not acquitted as a private person, but as our head, and believers are acquitted in his acquittance; nor was he accepted to a reward for his obedience as a private person, but as our head, and we are accepted to a reward in his acceptance. The Scripture teaches us, that when Christ was raised from the dead, he was justified; which justification as I have already shown, implies, both his acquittance from our guilt, and his acceptance to the exaltation and glory that was the reward of his obedience: but believers, as soon as they believe are admitted to partake with Christ in this his justification: hence we are told that he was "raised again for our justification" (Romans 4:25). (*Works* 19, 191)

This paragraph is perhaps the most important in the book. It provides one of the most concise summaries of the gospel Edwards gave in his ministry. It contains the raw material of the gospel, the truths which sinners must believe to be saved. Though we have discussed and will consider numerous essential matters related to conversion and true Christianity, there can be no real understanding of these truths unless one identifies the Bible's gospel message as the only means to conversion (see John 3; Romans 3–5). In the death of Christ for the salvation of the wicked, we discover the heart of salvation and the core content of true Christianity. Jesus has "taken man's guilt upon him" at the cross, dying in our place as a substitute to save us from hell and absorb the wrath of God for our sin. Because of His gift, one greater than any other we can conceive, "we are accepted" by God "to a reward," eternal life with God. This is the gospel. This is the foundation of Christian faith, the center of Edwards's preaching, and the point from which all other discussion of conversion flows.

In order to taste salvation, one must believe this gospel and not merely assent to it. Edwards spoke to this matter in numerous places, but rarely with more elegance and clarity than in his sermon "A Divine and Supernatural Light." In this sermon, he speaks of a fourth plank we might identify in his conversion theology, the "true sense" of holy things that marks the converted heart and that only comes from the influence of the Spirit:

> A TRUE SENSE OF THE DIVINE and superlative excellency of the things of religion; a real sense of the excellency of God, and Jesus Christ, and of the work of redemption, and the ways and works of God revealed in the gospel. There is a divine and superlative glory in these things; an excellency that is of a vastly higher kind, and more sublime nature, than in other things; a glory greatly distinguishing them

from all that is earthly and temporal. He that is spiritually enlightened truly apprehends and sees it, or has a sense of it. He don't merely rationally believe that God is glorious, but he has a sense of the gloriousness of God in his heart. There is not only a rational belief that God is holy, and that holiness is a good thing; but there is a sense of the loveliness of God's holiness. There is not only a speculatively judging that God is gracious, but a sense how amiable God is upon that account; or a sense of the beauty of this divine attribute. (*Works* 17, 413)

In one of the most famous passages from the entirety of his writings, Edwards went on to elegantly show how this "true sense" differs from a mere intellectual conviction:

THUS THERE IS A DIFFERENCE between having an opinion that God is holy and gracious, and having a sense of the loveliness and beauty of that holiness and grace. There is a difference between having a rational judgment that honey is sweet, and having a sense of its sweetness. A man may have the former, that knows not how honey tastes; but a man can't have the latter, unless he has an idea of the taste of honey in his mind. So there is a difference between believing that a person is beautiful, and having a sense of his beauty. The former may be obtained by hearsay, but the latter only by seeing the countenance. There is a wide difference

> between mere speculative, rational judging anything to be
> excellent, and having a sense of its sweetness, and beauty.
> The former rests only in the head, speculation only is con-
> cerned in it; but the heart is concerned in the latter. When
> the heart is sensible of the beauty and amiableness of a
> thing, it necessarily feels pleasure in the apprehension. It is
> implied in a person's being heartily sensible of the loveli-
> ness of a thing, that the idea of it is sweet and pleasant to
> his soul; which is a far different thing from having a
> rational opinion that it is excellent. (*Works* 17, 414)

The difference between a nominal faith that merely mimics
biblical Christianity and true faith is this "true sense" that the
pastor-theologian speaks of. The phrase itself compels our
attention, pairing as it does conviction, "true," and emotion,
"sense." Christianity as Edwards saw it—and as the Bible pic-
tures it—involves the sum total of one's mind and one's heart.
Head-knowledge without passion reduces Christianity to a
collection of interesting propositions. Though he did not cover
it here, heart-knowledge without truth reduces Christianity
to yet another religious experience. If the two combined,
though, an ideal balance could be struck.

When a person believes the gospel message, the things of
Christianity, of the Bible, and of church that once seemed so
ordinary compared to really interesting things—whether
celebrities or sports or movies or whatever else—now possess
a "glory greatly distinguishing them from all that is earthly and

temporal." In Edwards's biblical view, the person seized by the Spirit cannot see Christianity any longer in earthly terms. Like a butterfly that emerges from a cocoon, the converted sinner sees Christianity and its doctrines as things of beauty. Everything changes at this point for the redeemed person. Life overflows with God's goodness and beauty. The existence that once had no center—or that had a destructive one—now revolves around the person of Jesus Christ, whose work suddenly leaps off every page of the Bible and pours into every corner of life, calling the Christian to experience the joyful process of conformity to the divine will.

The Marks of True Conversion: Love for Christ

Edwards did not end his doctrine of conversion at this enlivening point, however. In his 1741 text *Distinguishing Marks of a True Work of the Spirit of God,* Edwards laid out a number of negative and positive signs that distinguished a true work of God from a false one. Though Edwards focused in this text on revivals more broadly, his words apply to individuals seeking to discern whether they know the Lord. Because we looked in the last chapter at several negative signs, aspects of religion that even devils might practice, we look here at the positive signs that indicate the presence of saving faith in the human heart.

The first of these signs was a "raised esteem" for Jesus Christ:

WHEN THAT SPIRIT that is at work amongst a people is observed to operate after such a manner, as to raise their esteem of that Jesus that was born of the Virgin, and was crucified without the gates of Jerusalem; and seems more to confirm and establish their minds in the truth of what the Gospel declares to us of his being the Son of God, and the Saviour of men; 'tis a sure sign that that spirit is the Spirit of God. This sign the Apostle gives us in the 1 John 4:2 and 1 John 4:3 verses, "Hereby know ye the Spirit of God; every spirit that confesseth that Jesus Christ is come in the flesh, is of God; and every spirit that confesseth not that Jesus Christ is come in the flesh, is not of God." This implies a confessing, not only that there was such a person that appeared in Palestine, and did and suffered those things that are recorded of him, but that that person was Christ, i.e. the Son of God, the Anointed of God to be Lord and Saviour, as the name Jesus Christ implies. That thus much is implied in the Apostle's meaning, is confirmed by the 1 John 4:15 verse, where the Apostle is still on the same subject of signs of the true Spirit: "Whosoever shall confess that Jesus is the Son of God, God dwelleth in him, and he in God." (*Works* 4, 249)

The point of this first sign is that when the Spirit moves in a person's heart and awakens them to faith and repentance, their view of Jesus changes. The Spirit "raise[s] their esteem" of Jesus and causes them to see that He is the Christ, "the Anointed of God to be Lord and Saviour." This recognition is not merely factual, of course, but involves both head and heart. This clarifies true Christianity. The nominal believer *respects* Jesus, but does not reverence or exalt Him. The true Christian takes delight in Jesus, a delight that is often palpable and contagious. When a persons claims saving faith, then, we should expect to see a "raised esteem" for Jesus Christ, the author of our redemption.

The Marks of True Conversion: Hatred of Sin

The second sign of a "true work" is an increased hatred for sin and defeat of sinful practices:

> WHEN THE SPIRIT THAT IS at work operates against the interest of Satan's kingdom, which lies in encouraging and establishing sin, and cherishing men's worldly lusts; this is a sure sign that 'tis a true, and not a false spirit. This sign we have given us in the 1 John 4:4 and 1 John 4:5 verses: "Ye are of God, little children, and have overcome them; because greater is he that is in you, than he that is in the world. They are of the world, therefore speak they of the world, and the world heareth them."

The pastor elaborated on this contention:

> SO THAT WE MAY SAFELY DETERMINE, from what the
> Apostle says, that the spirit that is at work amongst a
> people, that is observed to work after such a manner as to
> lessen men's esteem of the pleasures, profits and honors of
> the world, and to take off their hearts from an eager pur-
> suit after these things; and to engage them in a deep con-
> cern about a future and eternal happiness in, that invisible
> world, that the Gospel reveals; and puts them upon earnest
> seeking the kingdom of God and his righteousness; and
> convinces them of the dreadfulness of sin, the guilt that it
> brings, and the misery that it exposes to: I say, the spirit
> that operates after such a manner, must needs be the Spirit
> of God. (*Works* 4, 250–51).

This point, like the others, is both profound and simple. One
of the clear signs of a work of God is increased hatred for sin.
When the Spirit descends upon a human heart, He "lessen[s]
men's esteem of the pleasures, profits and honors of the
world," showing them "the dreadfulness of sin, the guilt that
it brings," and the "misery" that accrues to the unrepentant.
One's eyes are suddenly opened to see the dreadfulness of
one's condition. Where before one had spotted weaknesses
and flaws, but always had excuses at the ready to cover up
those personal blemishes, now the Spirit shows the sinner just

how degraded and evil he is. He realizes that he is wicked, separated from God, and that he must immediately kill sin, lest it kill him, and seek "the kingdom of God and his righteousness."

The Marks of True Conversion: Love for the Word

The third sign of a "true work" is a love for the Bible. Edwards tied this love for Scripture not to simple literary appreciation for its contents, but to a Spirit-given hunger and thirst for the Word of God:

THAT SPIRIT THAT OPERATES in such a manner, as to cause in men a greater regard to the Holy Scriptures, and establishes them more in their truth and divinity, is certainly the Spirit of God. This rule the Apostle gives us in the 1 John 4:6 verse: "We are of God; he that knoweth God heareth us: he that is not of God, heareth not us: hereby know we the spirit of truth and the spirit of error." "We are of God"—that is, "we the apostles, are sent forth of God, and appointed of him, to teach the world, and to deliver that doctrine, those instructions that are to be their rule; therefore he that knoweth God heareth us, etc." The Apostle's argument in the verse equally reaches all that in the same sense are of God, that is, all those that God has appointed and inspired to deliver to his church its rule of faith and practice; all the prophets and apostles, whose doctrine God has made the foundation on which he has built his church, as in Ephesians 2:20; all the penmen of the Holy Scriptures. The Devil never would go about to beget in persons a regard to that divine Word, which God hath given to be the great and standing rule for the direction of his church in all religious matters and concerns of their souls, in all ages. (*Works* 4, 253)

Many people respect the Bible. It is known as a "holy book," a sacred text. But few people view it as the actual word of God, that which God Himself "has appointed and inspired to deliver to his church its rule of faith and practice" as "the great and standing rule for the direction of his church." The Devil, according to Edwards, never impresses upon the human heart that the Bible possesses unparalleled "truth and divinity"; this only the Holy Spirit can do. Thus, where a person's heart flames with love and holy "regard" for the Scriptures, the Spirit has worked.

The Marks of True Conversion: Love for Truth and the Things of God

The fourth sign that marked the presence of a "true work" was a heightened love for truth and the things of God. Edwards continued:

AS FOR INSTANCE, if we observe that the spirit that is at work, makes men more sensible than they used to be, that there is a God, and that he is a great God, and a sin-hating God; and makes them more to realize it, that they must die, and that life is short, and very uncertain; and confirms persons in it that there is another world, that they have immortal souls, and that they must give account of themselves to God; and convinces them that they are exceeding sinful by nature and practice; and that they are helpless in themselves; and confirms them in other things that are agreeable to sound doctrine: the spirit that works thus, operates as a spirit of truth: he represents things as they are indeed: he brings men to the light; for whatever makes truth manifest, is light; as the Apostle Paul observes, Ephesians 5:13, "But all things that are reproved are made manifest by the light; for whatsoever doth make manifest is light." (*Works* 4, 254–55)

An awareness and responsiveness to divine truth was a clear signal that the Lord had moved in human hearts. So where people came to see "that there is a God" and that He is "great" and "sin-hating," and that they themselves have "immortal souls" and "must give account of themselves to God," the Spirit was working true conversion. As Edwards rightly noted, the Spirit does not lead believers into error. Therefore, when we hear news of conversion, whether mass or individual, we need to listen for resonances of the truth in the testimony of the convert. Do they love the truth more? Do they love God more? Do they subscribe to sound doctrine, and root their faith in it? Or is their faith based only on little more than sensations, experiences, impressions, and personal feelings? In our work to lift up biblical Christianity in our churches, we must emphasize that the children of God love His truth and abide in it.

The Marks of True Conversion:
Love for Believers

The final positive sign in Edwards's taxonomy of the Spirit's "true work" was love for one's fellow Christians. He declared:

IF THE SPIRIT THAT IS AT WORK among a people operates as a spirit of love to God [and] man, 'tis a sure sign that 'tis the Spirit of God. This sign the Apostle insists upon from the 1 John 4:7 verse to the end of the chapter: "Beloved, let us love one another; for love is of God, and everyone that loveth is born of God, and knoweth God. He that loveth not, knoweth not God, for God is love, etc." Here 'tis evident that the Apostle is still comparing those two sorts of persons that are influenced by the opposite kinds of spirits; and mentions love as a mark by which we may know who has the true spirit. But this is especially evident by the

> 1 John 4:12 and 1 John 4:13 verses: "If we love one another,
> God dwelleth in us, and his love is perfected in us. Hereby
> know we that we dwell in him, and he in us, because he
> hath given us of his Spirit." (*Works* 4, 255)

Many people who profess Christ lose their footing on this
final point. They may well appreciate fellow church members
and contribute in some way to their well-being, but they have
not been filled by the Lord with a holy love for fellow Christians, and thus they do not serve them. Spirit-given love that
transcends social, political, religious, or geographic common-
ality produces sacrifice for the good of one's fellow Christians,
as Galatians 6:10 instructs (this sacrificial service will regularly extend to unbelievers as well). True conversion will cause
stable couples to take in young Christians hungry for discipleship. It will lead Christians to give generously to missionaries and fellow believers (see 2 Corinthians 8). It will drive
older believers to spend time mentoring younger ones (see
Titus 2).

As the Scripture teaches, the healthy church, one filled
with true believers, bursts at the seams with love, whether
communicated from older women to young moms struggling
with the challenges of raising multiple tiny children, or from
college students intentionally spending time with elderly
members, or from a happily married couple reaching out to
another couple struggling with sin (see 1 Corinthians 13). In
these and many other ways, the true Christian, gifted with
love for fellow Christians, pushes beyond themselves and

their natural self-centeredness to bless the people around them—people with whom they may have nothing in common besides a mutual love of Christ (Galatians 3:27).

This is not a common standard by which people measure salvation today. If you ask a number of Christians how they know that they are saved, very few of them will reference the church and describe how they love people of all types now because of their unity in Christ. Edwards's words, however, direct us to closely involve the church in our doctrine of assurance. The way one cares for one's fellow members says more about our testimony of conversion than we might initially think. True Christians serve their fellow members out of love. This is a crucial mark of a saved soul and a missing element in many of our assemblies.

Embodying the Converted Life

The preceding offers valuable assistance to the modern church as we wrestle with the problem of nominalism. Each of Edwards's crucial contributions informs our own understanding of the biblical testimony on conversion. In sum, he shows us that the Christian life is the personal experience of God's grace and goodness. Though all of us will wrestle with sin until we go on to glory, the true Christian bears marks of conversion and offers the world a picture of a very different way of life. Though we live in a different age than Edwards, we would be wise to recover these marks in our churches as we stand for true Christianity.

We conclude with this powerful summation from Edwards's *Distinguishing Marks:*

THEREFORE WHEN THE SPIRIT that is at work amongst a people tends this way, and brings many of them to high and exalting thoughts of the divine Being, and his glorious perfections; and works in them an admiring, delightful sense of the excellency of Jesus Christ; representing him as "the chief among ten thousands, altogether lovely" [Canticles 5:10, Canticles 5:16], and makes him precious to the soul; winning and drawing the heart with those motives and incitements to love which the Apostle speaks of in that passage of Scripture we are upon, viz. the wonderful, free love of God in giving his only begotten Son to die for us, and the wonderful dying love of Christ to us, who had no love to him, but were his enemies; as vss. 1 John [4]:9 and 1 John [4]:10, "In this was manifested the love of God towards us, because that God sent his only begotten Son into the world, that we might live through him. Herein is love; not that we loved God, but that he loved us, and sent his Son to be the propitiation for our sins." (*Works* 4, 256)

Embracing True Christianity

Believe in Conversion and Do Not Assume the Gospel

*I*n working to support the cause of true Christianity, the first order of business for many of us is simply to refresh our belief in conversion. We need to remind ourselves that conversion exists. With Edwards, we need to find great joy in this fundamental reality. Though people doubt its existence, though discouraging signs abound in the church, yet God is God, and His Spirit moves where He wills it to go, saving whom He wills to save (John 3:8). Conversion is real, and we should treat it as such, whether in our homes, dealing with children, or among our friends. We must believe this in our hearts and teach it in our churches. This will enable us to push back doubt and despair that come not from God, the author of life, but from Satan, the enemy of the faith.

We must also never take the gospel for granted. We must identify the brief but essential content of the gospel as the ground of true conversion. In our churches, homes, and conversations with friends, we must not skate over the gospel, assuming that people understand and believe it. The gospel is the good news of salvation, the only means by which sinners can return to God (Romans 10). Its message of the salvation of sinners through Christ's atoning sacrifice and life-giving resurrection is the ground of faith and the core belief of all who truly know God. Churches filled with nominal Christians may well be those that talk little about the specifics of the gospel and its demands upon the lost, instead offering generalized versions of the message of salvation that require no real heart-change to accept. Salvation is simple, but it is driven by a definite message with clear content and a transformative call. We must preach this message constantly both personally as individuals and corporately in our churches, taking care that we never neglect the gospel and overlook its absolute necessity for salvation.

Seek the "True Sense"

*A*s we prioritize conversion in our circles, we need to emphasize that there is a vast difference between a mere profession of faith and a "true sense" of God's grace in Christ. It is by no means wrong to encourage people to respond to the gospel in a certain way. But we must take care that we do not confuse our hearers. Things like walking an aisle or raising a hand do not save one's soul. Only the "true sense" of the gospel, the sense that convinces the mind and awakens the heart, is salvific. We want people to taste this "true sense" of living faith that comes from genuine repentance from sin and love for Christ and His atoning work. We desire that sinners would not just come to church when it suits them, but that they would know the joy of a Spirit-filled life.

What can we do to create this kind of atmosphere? We

can start by defining and celebrating true conversion. If we offer sinners a vague, fuzzy, coddling Christianity, that is what they will respond to and live by, and many of them will not encounter the God of vibrant Christian faith. If we publicly exalt God and His work in Christ, we will greatly help our efforts to promote the true sense of converting grace. We want to see people who reinforce their confession of Christ by exhibiting love for God, hatred for sin, reverence for the Bible, a desire for truth, and unity with believers of all types and kinds.

Make the Church the Center of Christian Assurance

*T*oo many of us have missed the significance of the local church as what we might call the "factory of assurance." We have bought into individualist, man-centered Christianity that reduces faith to an isolated walk with God. In such a climate, we need to recover an Edwardsean model of church life in which the pastor disciples his people from the pulpit and delineates true faith from false faith. We need to build cultures of discipleship and corporate care in our churches, mirroring the early church as detailed in Acts 2. We should not automatically assume someone has genuinely come to Christ based only upon a one-time profession of faith, but should encourage them to immerse themselves in the local church and to lose themselves in the joys of sacrificial service in Christ's name. As they do so, we will be able to examine their lives and help them to see whether they have truly come to faith or not.

A common argument of many nominal Christians is that they love Jesus but don't care for the church. The teaching of 1 John exposes the flaws of this argument, revealing it to be an unbiblical dichotomy. All who are saved by God possess the Spirit, which links them to all other people who possess the Spirit. The local church, of course, is not perfect, and some have had difficult experiences with churches they have attended. But when God saves a person, He gives them a love for His people. His people are the church.

CHAPTER FOUR

Powerful Examples of True Christianity

$\mathcal{T}$he world is full of evil people. Their choices and actions are often devastating. If a person feeds their natural propensity for evil, they can wreak incredible havoc. History bears this out in abundance. We do not need to rack our brains to come up with examples of people who, having yielded fully to their wickedness, caused untold pain and suffering for many. In Hitler's Germany, Stalin's Russia, and Mao's China, we find examples of this terrible reality. Of course, beyond the ringleaders, the movement personalities, were untold people who had also committed their lives to the propagation of evil, not good. We do not and never will know many of their stories. History has absorbed their evil lives.

There are others from the past who have heard a different call. Some of this group are famous—people like Martin Luther, John Calvin, or John Wesley. These people gave themselves to a greater cause in a public arena. Others, however, lived quieter lives. In their own small corner of the world, they blazed a righteous course. Some taught Sunday school all of their lives and spent their own money on their students as they pointed them to Christ week by week. Others gave sacrificially to missions, skipping vacations to send another missionary to the field. Some Christians fought for racial and social justice in their communities, sharing the good news of Jesus even as they stood up for the oppressed when no one else would. Though these anonymous Christians received little earthly acclaim for their faithfulness to Christ, their good deeds are known to the Father.

This is the power of true Christianity. Though the number of true Christians may be small relative to the number of unbelievers (Matthew 7:13), God has made the world such that holiness stands out, inviting all to behold its beauty. Evil may entice people, drawing them in, but it never sparkles or shines. As he studied the Bible, Jonathan Edwards saw that had God designed the life of the true Christian to stun the eyes of the world with its brilliance. Conversion that was truly Christian resulted in holy living by regenerated sinners who savored and demonstrated the glory of the gospel.

In this chapter, we turn from Edwards's core conversionist beliefs to look at two personal examples of true Christianity as he conceived it. We discuss less and marvel more in this chapter as we look back at David Brainerd's work among the Native Americans from *The Life and Diary of David Brainerd* and the testimony of Abigail Hutchinson in the midst of terminal illness from *A Faithful Narrative of the Surprising Work of God.* These examples encourage us even as they call us to stand out for God in this sinful world.

The Missionary Heart of David Brainerd

David Brainerd was a young missionary to various Native American tribes whom Edwards took under his wing after Brainerd ran into trouble while in school at Yale, Edwards's *alma mater.* From an early age, Brainerd believed in the necessity of conversion, a conviction that landed him in trouble when he accused a Yale tutor of being unconverted. Though his zeal could get the best of him, Brainerd exhibited strong piety and a passion for the gospel. He clicked well with Edwards as a result. For his part, Edwards supported and mentored Brainerd, functioning as a father figure as Brainerd navigated the challenges of cross-cultural ministry to the Native Americans in Kaunaumee, NY, Easton, PA, and Cranbury, NJ. Brainerd died at a young age, likely from tuberculosis. In 1749, Edwards published Brainerd's diary after the young man passed away under the title *The Life and Diary of David Brainerd.* The book became a contemporary hit and a historic piece of missionary literature that has inspired thousands of Christians and missions workers.

In our brief coverage of Brainerd's life and witness, we

look chiefly at his love for the lost and his personal devotion to the Lord. At the same time, Brainerd struggled all his life with depression, a conflict that surfaces throughout his *Diary* in sections like this:

> WEDNESDAY, MAY 18. My circumstances are such that I have no comfort of any kind but what I have in God. I live in the most lonesome wilderness; have but one single person to converse with, that can speak English: Most of the talk I hear is either Highland Scotch or Indian. I have no fellow Christian to whom I might unbosom myself and lay open my spiritual sorrows, and with whom I might take sweet counsel in conversation about heavenly things, and join in social prayer. I live poorly with regard to the comforts of life: most of my diet consists of boiled corn, hasty pudding, etc. I lodge on a bundle of straw, and my labor is hard and extremely difficult; and I have little appearance of success to comfort me. The Indian affairs are very difficult; having no land to live on, but what the Dutch people lay claim to, and threaten to drive them off from; they have no regard to the souls of the poor Indians; and, by what I can learn, they hate me because I come to preach to 'em. But that which makes all my difficulties grievous to be born is that "God hides his face from me." (*Works* 7, 207)

Brainerd had resolved to take the gospel of Jesus Christ to a people many colonists neglected to their shame—the Native Americans (or "Indians" as he calls them). He had little shelter, little support, and little encouragement. He had a bright mind and a passionate heart, but he was not the kind of person one might pick out of a lineup to lead a great work of God.

As this quotation reflects, Brainerd fought relentlessly with his demons, and nearly succumbed to them at numerous points in his early missionary efforts. For month after month in his first few years of witness, he tells of days given over to sorrow and discouragement from the frustrations of failed missionary work. He had chosen to evangelize a pagan people who had no acquaintance with Christ. The darkness of their lives brought him immense pain. Fellowship was scarce. He had an interpreter, but found it difficult to connect with him over spiritual things. To summarize much of his early efforts, he saw no fruit, no tangible evidence of God's converting grace.

Despite his weaknesses and difficulties, however, he persevered out of devotion to the Lord. He kept trying to preach the gospel, even when he faltered in doing so:

> FRIDAY, DECEMBER 14. Near noon, went to the Indians; but knew not what to say to them, and was ashamed to look them in the face: I felt I had no power to address their consciences, and therefore had no boldness to say anything. Was, much of the day, in a great degree of despair about

ever doing or "seeing any good in the land of the living."
(*Works* 7, 278)

Days like this nearly sent Brainerd home. But after over a year
of sowing the gospel seed, the Native Americans stopped
ignoring him and began to take him seriously:

> SATURDAY, JUNE 29. Preached twice to the Indians; and
> could not but wonder at their seriousness and the strict-
> ness of their attention.—[*Journal*. Saw (as I thought) the
> hand of God very evidently, and in a manner somewhat
> remarkable, making provision for their subsistance
> together, in order to their being instructed in divine things.
> For this day and the day before, with only walking a little
> way from the place of our daily meeting, they killed three
> deer, which were a seasonable supply for their wants, and
> without which, it seems, they could not have subsisted
> together in order to attend the means of grace.] Blessed be
> God that has inclined their hearts to hear. And oh, how
> refreshing it is to me to see them attend with such uncom-
> mon diligence and affection, with tears in their eyes and
> concern in their hearts! In the evening, could not but lift up
> my heart to God in prayer, while riding to my lodgings:
> And blessed be his Name, had assistance and freedom. Oh,
> how much "better than life" is the presence of God! (*Works*
> 7, 301)

After a long period of spiritual drought, the Lord now honored Brainerd's work by opening the hearts of the lost. This continued as the work gained speed:

> AUGUST 5. After a sermon had been preached by another minister, I preached and concluded the public work of the solemnity from John 7:37, and in my discourse addressed the Indians in particular, who sat by themselves in a part of the house; at which time one or two or them were struck with deep concern, as they afterwards told me, who had been little affected before: others had their concern increased to a considerable degree. In the evening (the greater part of them being at the house where I lodged) I discoursed to them and found them universally engaged about their soul's concern, inquiring what they should do to be saved. And all their conversation among themselves turned upon religious matters, in which they were much assisted by my interpreter, who was with them day and night.
>
> This day there was one woman, that had been much concerned for her soul ever since she first heard me preach in June last, who obtained comfort, I trust, solid and well grounded: She seemed to be filled with love to Christ, at the same time behaved humbly and tenderly, and appeared afraid of nothing so much as of grieving and offending him whom her soul loved. (*Works* 7, 306)

As a group, the Native Americans were awakening. Concern for their souls spread from person to person, such that Brainerd and his interpreter had to devote many hours to spiritual counsel. Brainerd had even seen some profess faith, including the woman he mentions above, who "seemed to be filled with love to Christ." Brainerd's perseverance was paying off.

The Rewards of Brainerd's Perseverance

The work which once seemed in danger of dying out in abject failure now flared to life with such dynamism that Brainerd could scarcely manage it. One summer day's investment loomed large in the missionary's mind:

> AUGUST 16. Spent considerable time in conversing privately with sundry of the Indians. Found one that had got relief and comfort after pressing concern, and could not but hope, when I came to discourse particularly with her, that her comfort was of the right kind.
>
> In the afternoon, preached to them from John 6:26–34. Toward the close of my discourse, divine truths were attended with considerable power upon the audience, and more especially after public service was over, when I particularly addressed sundry distressed persons.

This preaching caused quite a response among Brainerd's hearers:

THERE WAS A GREAT CONCERN for their souls spread pretty generally among them: But especially there were two persons newly awakened to a sense of their sin and misery, one of whom was lately come, and the other had all along been very attentive, and desirous of being awakened, but could never before have any lively view of her perishing state. But now her concern and spiritual distress was such, that I thought I had never seen *any* more pressing. Sundry old men were also in distress for their souls; so that they could not refrain from weeping and crying out aloud, and their bitter groans were the most convincing as well as affecting evidence of the reality and depth of their inward anguish. God is powerfully at work among them! True and genuine convictions of sin are daily promoted in many instances, and some are newly awakened from time to time; although some few, who felt a commotion in their passions in days past, seem now to discover that their hearts were never duly affected. I never saw the work of God appear so independent of means as at this time. (*Works* 7, 314–16)

Brainerd's faithful preaching of the gospel paid off. His zeal for the gospel and concern for souls, marks of true Christianity, led him to push through hardship and repeatedly witness to the Native Americans. Because he did so, he saw the Lord work in miraculous ways among this people. Dozens came to faith under Brainerd's watch, with the awakening among the lost reaching such a height that the missionary commented that he "never saw the work of God" show itself "so independent of [human] means." In true Edwardsean fashion, Brainerd observed that many people experienced deep "distress for their souls" as "true and genuine convictions of sin" spread to many, including some who had thought themselves saved but now realized "that their hearts were never duly affected." The true preaching of the Word had led to true marks of conversion, sweeping away both pagan lostness and nominal Christianity among the people.

The young man died not long after this exciting event before he reached thirty years of age. He never fully defeated depression, and he knew his struggles, but he died a victorious Christian, one who had given his life to promote the gospel and who had, despite considerable personal weaknesses, persevered in his own walk with Christ until the end. He did not die then in fame or earthly glory. In time, however, his example would help inspire a worldwide evangelical missions movement that led thousands of people from a wide range of denominations to carry the gospel to millions separated from God. Though he found happiness in the Edwards home and in a sweet kinship with Jerusha Edwards, Brainerd was a lonely soul who doggedly went into the wild to witness to pagan tribes. In a manner that speaks volumes today, he picked up his cross and carried it, stopping only when illness and exhaustion ended his earthly labor.

As we pursue true Christianity, we should seek to be believers who have a Brainerd-like commitment to the gospel of Christ and who are willing to lay down their lives to reach those estranged from God in places near and far. All who do so will like Brainerd leave a testimony that cannot help but inspire others to do the same in a world desperate for hope.

The Touching Account of
Abigail Hutchinson's Devotion

Edwards found inspiring examples of true Christianity not only in missionaries on the field but in members of his own flock. In his Northampton congregation, Jonathan Edwards witnessed many dramatic conversions. Few, however, impressed themselves on his soul more than the salvation of Abigail Hutchinson, a young woman who suffered from a terminal illness. In his *Faithful Narrative of the Surprising Work of God*, Edwards recounted Hutchinson's conversion and subsequent love for God with moving prose.

Edwards began with the young woman's background:

SHE WAS OF A RATIONAL understanding family: there could be nothing in her education that tended to enthusiasm, but rather to the contrary extreme. 'Tis in no wise the temper of the family to be ostentatious of experiences, and it was far from being her temper. She was before her conversion, to the observation of her neighbors, of a sober and inoffensive conversation; and was a still, quiet, reserved person. She had long been infirm of body, but her infirmity

had never been observed at all to incline her to be notional
or fanciful, or to occasion anything of religious melancholy.
She was under awakenings scarcely a week, before there
seemed to be plain evidence of her being savingly converted. (*Works* 4, 192)

After her brother spoke to her about the gospel, Abigail became frightened about her spiritual condition. She could not
shake thoughts about her sin, according to Edwards, and thus
came to a crisis point in her spirituality:

HER GREAT TERROR, she said, was that she had sinned
against God. Her distress grew more and more for three
days; until (as she said) she saw nothing but blackness of
darkness before her, and her very flesh trembled for fear of
God's wrath: she wondered and was astonished at herself,
that she had been so concerned for her body, and had
applied so often to physicians to heal that, and had neglected her soul. Her sinfulness appeared with a very awful
aspect to her, especially in three things, viz. her original sin,
and her sin in murmuring at God's providence, in the
weakness and afflictions she had been under, and in want
of duty to parents, though others had looked upon her to
excel in dutifulness. On Saturday, she was so earnestly
engaged in reading the Bible and other books that she continued in it, searching for something to relieve her, till her

eyes were so dim that she could not know the letters. Whilst she was thus engaged in reading, prayer, and other religious exercises, she thought of those words of Christ, wherein he warns us not to be as the heathen, that think they shall be heard for their much speaking [Matthew 6:7]; which, she said, led her to see that she had trusted to her own prayers and religious performances, and now she was put to a non-plus, and knew not which way to turn herself, or where to seek relief. (*Works* 4, 192–93)

A few days later, Abigail found rest from her fear and doubt. She turned to the comforting voice of Scripture, finding encouragement for her penitent heart:

ON THE SABBATH DAY she was so ill that her friends thought it not best that she should go to public worship, of which she seemed very desirous: but when she went to bed on the Sabbath-day night, she took up a resolution that she would the next morning go to the minister, hoping to find some relief there. As she awaked on Monday morning, a little before day, she wondered within herself at the easiness and calmness she felt in her mind, which was of that kind which she never felt before; as she thought of this, such words as these were in her mind: "The words of the Lord are pure words, health to the soul and marrow to the bones." And then these words came to her mind, "The blood

of Christ cleanses [us] from all sin" [1 John 1:7]; which were
accompanied with a lively sense of the excellency of Christ,
and his sufficiency to satisfy for the sins of the whole world.
She then thought of that expression, "'tis a pleasant thing
for the eyes to behold the sun" [Ecclesiastes 11:7]; which
words then seemed to her to be very applicable to Jesus
Christ. By these things her mind was led into such con-
templations and views of Christ, as filled her exceeding full
of joy. (*Works* 4, 193)

Now that Abigail had discovered the satisfaction and relief
that comes through repentance and faith in the name of the
Savior, she devoted herself to living for the Lord with the time
she had left. It was not long.

Abigail made the most of her days, focusing herself on
the grace of God, witnessing to whomever she could, living
happily despite her inability to eat solid food and sustain her
body. Edwards recorded a number of evidences of the young
woman's changed heart, some of which are deeply moving:

AT THE LAST TIME on Wednesday morning, while in the
enjoyment of a spiritual view of Christ's glory and fulness,
her soul was filled with distress for Christless persons, to
consider what a miserable condition they were in: and she
felt in herself a strong inclination immediately to go forth
to warn sinners; and proposed it the next day to her

brother to assist her in going from house to house; but her brother restrained her, by telling her of the unsuitableness of such a method. She told one of her sisters that day that she loved all mankind, but especially the people of God. Her sister asked her why she loved all mankind. She replied because God had made them. After this, there happened to come into the shop where she was at work, three persons that were thought to have been lately converted; her seeing them as they stepped in one after another into the door so affected her, and so drew forth her love to them, that it overcame her, and she almost fainted: and when they began to talk of the things of religion, it was more than she could bear; they were obliged to cease on that account. (*Works* 4, 194)

We see that Abigail demonstrated clear signs of conversion. Primarily, she had a grave concern for unrepentant sinners, one of the strongest marks of true Christianity. Many people can pretend to have love for God. They can say the right things and go to the right events. But far fewer nominal believers will express concern for the eternal fate of the lost. Lukewarm believers won't want to think about such things, for doing so will raise the question of their own salvation. Abigail's evangelistic heart showed that she loved the Lord. Such concern is an important mark of true Christianity.

Abigail's delight centered in the God she loved. In a

manner common among associates of Edwards, she sometimes lost herself in contemplation of the divine, experiencing blissful joy in the Lord:

> SHE HAD MANY EXTRAORDINARY discoveries of the glory of God and Christ; sometimes, in some particular attributes, and sometimes in many. She gave an account that once, as those four words passed through her mind, "wisdom," "justice," "goodness," and "truth," her soul was filled with a sense of the glory of each of these divine attributes, but especially the last; "truth," said she, "sunk the deepest!" And therefore as these words passed, this was repeated, "Truth, truth!" Her mind was so swallowed up with a sense of the glory of God's truth and other perfections, that she said it seemed as though her life was going, and that she saw it was easy with God to take away her life by discoveries of himself. Soon after this she went to a private religious meeting. . . . Afterwards she was greatly affected, and rejoiced with these words, "Worthy is the Lamb that was slain" [Revelation 5:12]. (*Works* 4, 194–95)

Even though Abigail's faith was young, she had acquired a theocentric worldview from the start. She had no affinity for the trappings of religion. The desperation of her physical condition intensified her love for the Lord, sharpening it in a powerful way. In her waning hours, Abigail had a "sense and view of the glory of God all the time." The dying young woman's strength began to fail, but her affection for Christ did not. Though we must not idealize her, we can admire her and honor her by letting her example fuel our own love for the Lord.

Abigail gave perhaps her most moving demonstration of trust in the Savior in her final days. In words that must have been difficult to write, Edwards described the final deterioration of her condition and the beauty of her faith. The final account is richly edifying and worth quoting at length:

> HER ILLNESS IN THE LATTER PART of it was seated much in her throat; and swelling inward, filled up the pipe so that she could swallow nothing but what was perfectly liquid, and but very little of that, and with great and long strug-glings and stranglings, that which she took in flying out at her nostrils till she at last could swallow nothing at all. She had a raging appetite to food, so that she told her sister, when talking with her about her circumstances, that the worst bit that she threw to her swine would be sweet to her: but yet when she saw that she could not swallow it, she seemed to be as perfectly contented without it, as if she had no appetite to it. Others were greatly moved to see what she underwent, and were filled with admiration at her unexampled patience. At a time when she was striving in vain to get down a little food, something liquid, and was

very much spent with it, she looked up on her sister with a smile, saying, "O Sister, this is for my good!" At another time, when her sister was speaking of what she underwent, she told her that she lived an heaven upon earth for all that. She used sometimes to say to her sister, under her extreme sufferings, "It is good to be so!" Her sister once asked her why she said so. "Why," says she, "because God would have it so: It is best that things should be as God would have 'em: it looks best to me." (*Works* 4, 197)

Abigail persevered in her faith until the very end, painful as it was:

SHE WAS VERY WEAK a considerable time before she died, having pined away with famine and thirst, so that her flesh seemed to be dried upon her bones; and therefore could say but little, and manifested her mind very much by signs. She said she had matter enough to fill up all her time with talk, if she had but strength. A few days before her death, some asked her whether she held her integrity still, whether she was not afraid of death. She answered to this purpose, that she had not the least degree of fear of death. They asked her why she would be so confident. She answered, "If I should say otherwise, I should speak con-trary to what I know: there is," says she, "indeed a dark

entry, that looks something dark, but on the other side
there appears such a bright shining light, that I cannot be
afraid!" She said not long before she died that she used to
be afraid how she should grapple with death; but, says she,
"God has shewed me that he can make it easy in great
pain." Several days before she died, she could scarcely say
anything but just yes, and no, to questions that were asked
her, for she seemed to be dying for three days together; but
seemed to continue in an admirable sweet composure of
soul, without any interruption, to the last, and died as a
person that went to sleep, without any struggling, about
noon, on Friday, June 27, 1735. (*Works* 4, 198)

Hundreds of years later, we feel the pain of this young
woman's death. Her life plays out on paper as something like
a tragedy. A young life, so full of joy and beauty, taken at its
most promising point, just when faith had caught fire. On
closer examination, though, we see that the Lord had a special plan for Abigail. It was not her calling to live long, but it
was her calling to live well. Abigail experienced the delights of
true conversion and drew all eyes to God's work.

We do well to take note of how she suffered. So many of
us allow ourselves to grow depressed over matters far smaller
than a terminal disease. We complain, whether directly or
through passive-aggressive speech, forgetting the testimony
of people like Abigail Hutchinson. Her example calls us to
emulate her and to bear up under suffering and use it to glorify

God. To do so, we will have to shift our outlook on this life. Many of us, after all, do not have a terminal illness to bring us face to face with our faith. But if we would take stock of our lives and evaluate them to see what marks of conversion we possess, we would set ourselves up to live life with abandon and leave a testimony like Abigail Hutchinson, who pursued and tasted the riches of true Christianity and whose memory calls others to do the same.

Incarnating True Christianity

Conversion, as we saw in the last chapter, is real. But not only in a theological sense, such that we can formulate and understand it. Conversion has a definite look and feel. It does not mute one's natural personality or even sweep away all one's sins. But it does make a person new. Examples of people like David Brainerd and Abigail Hutchinson prove this, as do many others from Edwards's writings and from our own experiences. Brainerd and Hutchinson are not "all-stars," after all, but humble, ordinary people saved by the grace of God who lived extraordinary lives due to their pursuit of the Savior. Their lives modeled the doctrines taught by the Northampton pastor, showing us today that his picture of Christianity is not unreachable but is within our own grasp as well.

We have not looked at the lives of these two to put them on a pedestal. Instead, we have seen what true Christianity can look like when the heart and mind embrace the gospel and allow it to reshape human existence. The gospel comes to us as a message, but it transcends simple propositions and statements. It is a living force, and when it meets with a repentant, committed heart, it makes all things new (2 Corinthians 5:17). Physical beauty and the trappings of wealth may naturally draw our eyes, but the beauty of holiness, sparked from true conversion initiated by the power of the Holy Spirit, shines with a brilliance not seen in anything else in this world.

The lives of David and Abigail ended long ago, but their examples live on. They urge us today to recognize the power of true conversion and the potency of a life devoted in entirety to the work of God. Both of these young people struggled with physical weakness and sickness. Neither had an easy road. But where so many of us give in to our sin and obstacles, these two persevered, seeking the face of God. They are examples for us, Christians whom we must remember as we seek true conversion and holy passion in our own ordinary, conflicted, possibility-filled lives.

Embracing True Christianity

Embody Vibrant Christianity in Trial or Comfort

*T*he preceding biographies offer us encouragement. As we have seen at other places in our study of Edwards's life and work, the individual committed to God can do great things for Him. This applies to all types of persons. We do not need to be a theological giant, a pastor, or to be free of physical weakness or various forms of illness. Both of the people studied in this chapter suffered daily from bodily sickness. The work of the kingdom, we see, is very different from the world of business or politics. God uses people of all types and takes special pleasure in glorifying His name through the weak: "God chose what is weak in the world to shame the strong," wrote the Apostle Paul in the first century, and the same truth applies today (1 Corinthians 1:27). Though we so often think that we need to choose the same people to lead us that the world would choose—the strong, charming, highly intelligent, and ambitious—we must remember that the Lord frequently uses the weak and lowly to do great things for Him. The gospel welcomes and enfranchises all people. Those whom others would shun have often played a leading role in the advancement of the kingdom—a crucial truth that we must not forget. The weak are not disadvantaged when it comes to displaying the strength of true Christianity. The absence of abundance allows them to display Christ all the more.

Our Lord's own ministry triumphed not through the force of His personality, or the sheer attractiveness of His person, but through the power of God in the weakness of human flesh. Every Christian, however weak or strong, has the opportunity to serve in the role the Lord has given them, whether it is located in a far-off mission field, a home filled with children, a crisis-pregnancy center, the floor of the U.S. Senate, a baseball team, a large corporation, a cleaning business, or a hospital bed. True Christianity as embodied by all types of Christians beams into every sphere it enters.

Help Every Member to Serve and Contribute

*T*his has implications for our churches. As we emphasize true Christianity, we should work hard to place our members in positions of service. As Abigail's example reminds us, people of all abilities and situations serve on the front lines of the gospel. In the introduction, we referenced nameless Christians who have done great things for God. This is not just inspiring fiction. Our pastors and teachers play the most prominent role in our congregations, but the church would not work without countless people giving their time and energy to serve. In addition, many of our pastors and leaders cannot meet non-Christians on a daily basis like others in the congregation can. Each member has a vital role to play in the kingdom of God.

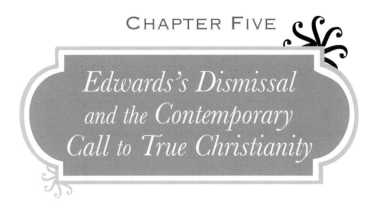

CHAPTER FIVE

Edwards's Dismissal and the Contemporary Call to True Christianity

*I*n an ideal world, good always wins. We see this in many popular movies. Despite great obstacles, the hero generally defeats the bad guys, rescues the girl, and saves the planet. Order and peace return, celebration ensues, and everyone lives happily ever after.

But real life plays by different rules. Sometimes good—and people working for good—win out, and sometimes they don't. From a Christian perspective, sometimes our virtuous undertakings go well and sometimes they fall short. There is no guarantee in this fallen world that God's people will always prevail or that people living in error will magically adopt truth once it is presented to them. In His providence, God does what He deems is best, producing effects in our lives that we do not always desire and sometimes cannot figure out.

The case of Jonathan Edwards and his congregation fits this premise to a tee. Edwards was his era's most famous pastor, and Northampton was a prominent town with a well-known assembly, the First Church. As we have seen, Edwards exercised a stoutly theological ministry at the church punctuated by revivals and fueled by artful sermons filled with creative and profound thought. As a preacher, Edwards is unequaled in American history; as a theologian, Edwards has no peer in this country. Yet strange as it sounds, the Northampton church fired Edwards twenty years into his pastorate, dismissing him for his handling of what is known as the "Communion Controversy."

We will look briefly at this affair in this chapter, observing that this struggle emerged from Edwards's deep concern over nominal Christianity in his church. Conversion was never theoretical for the pastor; it was always practical, a matter of first concern. He could not abide a church situation so evidently infected with lukewarmness. Though the conflict did not end happily or sinlessly for either side, Edwards's example instructs us today to seek true conversion in our churches.

Once we have discussed this matter, we will conclude by returning to the present day. Aware that each of us has faults and weaknesses, we will suggest several steps that the modern church might take to renew itself. Our Edwardsean solution will propose a number of points that Christians today can use in their quest to promote true Christianity.

The Communion Controversy

Edwards had long disliked the Northampton church's policy on communion that his grandfather, Solomon Stoddard, had instituted. Stoddard, who had pastored the church for fifty-five years before Edwards, saw the sacrament as a "converting ordinance" and thus welcomed all who professed faith and lived decently to take the cup and bread. Edwards had disagreed with his grandfather on this point for decades before he went public with his own view—that only those who lived holy lives could take the sacrament. Edwards spoke of his initial hesitancy to change the policy in 1749:

> I HAVE FORMERLY BEEN of [Stoddard's] opinion, which I imbibed from his books, even from my childhood, and have in my proceedings conformed to his practice; though never without some difficulties in my view, which I could not solve: yet, however, a distrust of my own understanding, and deference to the authority of so venerable a man, the seeming strength of some of his arguments, together with the success he had in his ministry, and his great reputation and influence, prevailed for a long time to bear down my scruples. (*Works* 12, 169)

In the 1740s, however, Edwards felt he could no longer allow people to take communion who refused to demonstrate by their lifestyle their profession of faith. The pastor did not want to limit communion only to the most spiritually vibrant people in his congregation; he merely wanted to emphasize true conversion in a biblical manner and allow people to take it who lived in a godly way. Edwards thought that this position, grounded in a strong scriptural argument, had the high ground. Instead, the new policy soon crumbled beneath his feet, taking him with it.

Edwards outlined his views in *Lectures on the Qualifications for Full Communion in the Church of Christ*. There, he advanced his view that only professing Christians with evident piety should take the sacrament:

> 'TIS PLAIN BY THE SCRIPTURE, and 'tis owned on all sides, that those who are admitted to the communion of the Christian church must be visible saints. All allow that, which is at once granting the very point in question, for to be visible saints is to be visibly godly men. To be a saint is to be a godly man, and to be visibly a saint is to be visibly a godly man; and to be visibly so is to be so in appearance to the eyes of men: it is to be a godly man as far as men can see and judge.

Undercutting the counter-argument that no one could truly know a person's spiritual state, Edwards offered a clear refutation, pointing out that authentic belief naturally produced evident piety:

VISIBILITY HAS RELATION to reality. Everything that is visibly gold is not real gold, but that which is gold visibly is real gold to appearance and acceptance. 'Tis so in everything. There are visibly good men and really good men; there are visibly honest men and really honest men. Now there are more men that are visibly honest men than are really so, but he that is visibly an honest man is to appear, or as to what is visible to others, really an honest man. So he that is visibly another man's child [is, to appearance, that man's child]. So he that is visibly a saint is, to appearance and to the eye and judgment of men, really a saint. (*Works* 25, 357)

The controversy over spiritual requirements for communion bled over into church membership. When a young man came to him in 1748 seeking admission to the church, Edwards requested a narrative of his conversion. This emphasis went hand-in-hand with his views on communion, recently made public. As with communion, Edwards believed that church membership and its privileges were for true Christians, not those professing faith but not living it. When some protested this decision and his position on the Lord's Supper, Edwards, probably unwisely, published not one but two books outlining and defending his understanding of the subject. His argument for pure church membership mirrored his argument for true believers' communion:

'TIS MOST MANIFEST by the Scripture, and what none denies or disputes, that none ought to be admitted into the Christian church but professing Christians. But they that make no profession of godliness, they are not professors of the Christian religion in the Scripture sense. The Christian religion is the religion of Christ, or the religion that Jesus Christ came to teach. But the religion that Christ taught consisted mainly in true piety of heart and life. Indeed, the custom of the present day has called something else the religion of Christ besides this: 'tis customary to call the doctrines of Christianity the Christian religion. But that is nothing to the purpose; the question is what the Scripture represents as the Christian religion, what the Bible informs us is the religion of Jesus Christ.

Christianity was a "heart religion," said Edwards, not a code of ethics or body of abstract doctrines that one committed to and then forgot:

THE SCRIPTURE TEACHES that the religion of Jesus Christ is heart religion, a spiritual religion. The worship that Christ came to teach was worshipping in spirit and in truth. Now in order to men's professing the religion of Jesus Christ, men must profess that which is the religion of Jesus Christ. But if men profess only the doctrines of religion and the

outward services, and leave out what is spiritual, the thing
that they profess is not the religion of Jesus Christ, because
the most essential things that belong to his religion are left
out. To profess a very small part of Christianity only, is not
to profess Christianity. (*Works* 25, 359)

The result of a relaxed policy on church membership that did
not prioritize a vibrant Christian walk would prove disastrous
not only to the church but to Christianity more broadly:

TO MAKE A PUBLIC profession of common, superficial religion at the same time that a man don't pretend to the inter-
nal, is in effect to make an open profession of being
lukewarm, and so more hateful to Christ than a heathen.
And who can believe that Christ, by his own institution,
has appointed such a profession as this to be the terms of
being received into his church and family and to his table
as his friends and children? (*Works* 25, 360)

Edwards's arguments possessed clarity and force, but many did
not receive them well. The controversy begun over communion and extended over membership stretched over many
months, with people from all over New England listening for
details of the Edwards-First Church divide. In the end,
Edwards failed to rally enough supporters to his side. With several previous conflicts in the background that still simmered

between Edwards and his detractors, the church fired him on June 22, 1750.

As covered in *Jonathan Edwards: Lover of God*, these events disordered Edwards's life and brought many trials to his family. He continued to minister in Northampton for a time as the interim pastor, but no happy resolution came of his situation.

The pastor's stance on true Christianity cost him dearly. Yet in Edwards's mind, this issue was of such importance that he was willing to put everything—his reputation, his pastorate, his personal comfort—on the line. He believed that in advocating for believer's communion, he was helping to win the lost and stamp the church as the holy outpost of God. He took personal responsibility for the advancement of true Christianity. His conception of the pastorate, articulated in his farewell sermon to the church, sheds light on his actions in the controversies over communion and membership:

MINISTERS ARE SET AS GUIDES and teachers, and are rep-resented in Scripture as lights set up in the churches; and in the present state meet their people from time to time in order to instruct and enlighten them, to correct their mistakes, and to be a voice behind them, saying, "This is the way, walk in it" [Is. 30:21]; to evince and confirm the truth by exhibiting the proper evidences of it, and to refute errors and corrupt opinions, to convince the erroneous and establish the doubting. (*Works* 25, 466)

With his conception of the church, Edwards could not countenance lukewarm practice in the areas of communion or
membership. With his conception of his own role as shepherd
of his members' souls, he could not stand by as people idled
spiritually, allowing the gospel to go in one ear and out the
other, as if the good news of God were nothing more than a
passing thought. The gospel as Edwards saw it was a searing
light that bore into sinful humanity and forever altered it.
Upon this conception of the gospel and Christianity Edwards
banked all of his pastoral ministry. Other factors emerged that
complicated the Northampton situation, but at base, the communion controversy boiled down to different understandings
of Christianity. Though he at times fanned the flames of controversy with his manner of handling disagreements, in this
matter Edwards took a sound position. Biblical fidelity on this
point did not translate to congregational unity, however, leaving one of history's most faithful pastors to retreat to the
wilderness.

Embracing True Christianity

Though Edwards never returned to the same kind of
pulpit ministry he had in Northampton, his pastoral and theological legacy lives on. We have traced his doctrine of conversion in this volume, peppering it with examples from his
life and the lives of others to show that it was no figment of

his spiritual imagination. We now seek to apply the insights and practical experience of Edwards to our modern context. Though this is by no means an exhaustive proposal, it is a call to arms to Christians everywhere to seek true conversion and the vivifying life it creates.

A Theocentric Approach to Life, Ministry, and the Gospel

*A*t the center of Edwards's understanding of conversion was his view of God. God had the preeminence—He created life, He founded the church, He saved souls, He deserved obedience and faith. Edwards's ministry centered not around pragmatic questions, but around a dominant concern that all that he would do and say would bring glory to God and advance His kingdom. God, not statistics or personal reputation, occupied center stage in his mind. Edwards knew that he did not need to please man; he needed to please God. He followed the theocentric trail wherever it led him, even when it led into territory that threatened to harm his ministry due to the lack of scriptural understanding in his church. When he lost his job, he did not blame God. His zeal for a ministry that honored the Lord persisted through great trial. Life was not about him, after all. It centered around God and His glory. This outlook grounded Edwards in happy seasons and buoyed him in times of difficulty.

In the deepest part of his soul, Edwards believed that the Lord had called him to labor for true conversion. Theocentric ministry in the name of Christ to a fallen world meant that sinners had to learn about their desperate state. This meant calling hostile sinners to account, a matter to which the Northampton pastor devoted considerable attention. Edwards spent great amounts of time and energy pleading with nominal Christians who hid beneath a surface Christianity to recognize the self-deception of their hearts. Edwards could not pretend that all was well in his church and go blithely about his business while members of his church scrambled to sit in more impressive pews and approached the communion table with nothing but a veneer of godliness. Edwards rose to meet these challenges. He did so even when it could—and did— cost him everything.

What can we learn from Edwards's approach today? Looking back to the first chapter, the world in which we live and minister is very similar to Edwards's. Though America as a nation makes few claims about any kind of Christian identity today, many of our churches have drawn people who for one reason or another claim conversion but whose lives fail to measure up to true Christianity (as we saw in chapter 1). In such a setting, with all kinds of financial and social pressures, it is difficult for many pastors to imagine confronting their people with the need to be converted and to reckon with lukewarm Christianity. But this is precisely what lukewarm Christians need. If the material from the first chapter shows us anything, it is that many professing Christians are floundering. They know basically nothing about the Bible or Christianity, they struggle to attend church, they hold beliefs in direct contradiction to the Scripture, and they neither witness nor have even the most basic success in educating their children in the things of God. This is a frightening situation.

A theocentric ministry demands that our Christian leaders shake off all of the distractions and lesser cares of their vocation and, in the most fundamental sense, rededicate their ministries to the Lord. The historic model of the pastor-theologian offers us an excellent antidote to our weakened pastorates in which theology is a bad word and preaching is group therapy. We don't advocate for a theocentric ministry merely so that people will get right with God. The first reason to locate one's mission in God is because this brings Him glory. This may sound rather ordinary or obvious to some. In our day, however, many have lost sight of it.

Ministry, as with all of Christianity, is fundamentally about God. It is derived from and dependent upon His Word. The Scripture is authoritative over everything and it is sufficient for all of ministry. This does not mean that all one does is quote Scripture. One needs to preach the Word and live it out with passion in order to draw sinners to salvation. This is what the church needs. We do not need to follow secular business practices to win lost souls. We need our churches to promote and embody true conversion in all its power and attractiveness. Though we can surely glean wisdom from other sources, the Word gives us all that we need to honor God in our congregations. It is not a springboard, a suggestion box, or an outmoded text. It is the mind and counsel of the Almighty given to us to form and direct our ministry in His name.

This also applies to lay Christians who love their churches and want to spread authentic Christianity. In whatever church setting we find ourselves, all of us must act as agents of true Christianity and students of the Word. As we noted in chapter 4, every Christian serves on the "front lines" of ministry. All of us have the opportunity to cultivate and model robust biblical thinking and living. Indeed, if Edwards had had more laypeople who bucked the status quo and joined him in his righteous quest for authentic spirituality, this book would tell a far happier tale. The pastor cannot go it alone; he needs the assistance of his people.

A Belief in the Centrality of the Gospel-Driven Church

*T*he work of Edwards shows that he believed in the centrality of the local church. He saw it as the place where true Christianity took visible shape and God incarnated His gospel. He took church membership seriously and labored to create a situation in which all who belonged to his congregation and observed the sacraments held true love for Christ in their hearts. He gave himself to the work of the church and labored to spread the riches of the biblical witness before his people. In sum, Edwards loved the church and drove himself hard to bless and build it.

We need today to recover an Edwardsean understanding of the church. We need to see it as the outpost of God, and we need our ministers to see themselves as "lights set up in the churches" to point people to God. We need to see the church as the place where true Christians live and work, calling those outside to the light of the gospel that emanates from their assembly. We need our churches to teach the full counsel of Scripture so that believers will know the Bible and be able to incorporate it into their lives. We need our teaching and preaching to center around the gospel to the point that unbelievers visiting our churches have trouble staying in unrepentant sin. Though we want unbelievers and nominal Christians to feel welcome in our churches and loved by our people, we do not want them to be able to play fast and loose with God. We want them to come into constant contact with the gospel such that they will realize their desperate plight and reckon with their sin. We want them to know, above all, that the church is not just another organization, another club to join and profit from, but is a holy movement of God's Spirit that calls people not to be served, but to serve, to lay down their lives in order to glorify God and fulfill His purpose for humanity (following Christ's example—see Matthew 20:28 and Mark 10:45). This may well mean that we need to take a hard look at our membership roles to see just how many of our members attend, let alone serve, the church.

We need as well to recognize that some have transferred their affection from the church to other institutions. The twentieth century witnessed the rise of numerous parachurch ministries that have, in many ways, greatly aided the evangelical movement. Many of these organizations perform vital functions and offer sound teaching that draws the lost and blesses the people of God. Yet in some instances, Christians have devoted their time and attention to parachurch ministries rather than the local church.

In such a culture, we must emphasize that the church is not a mere option for believers, an entity that one may shape as one sees fit and align with if one desires. It is the gathering of God's people designed by Him to shepherd them through a world in which Satan seeks to devour and kill. The church is not incidental to true Christianity; it is essential to the sustenance of a Spirit-filled heart.

A Concern for Nominal Christians of Specific Types

*E*dwards did not simply lash out against nominal Christianity. He came against it from various angles, addressing specific temptations and circumstances. We saw this demonstrated in his handling of the pew controversy, where he challenged wealthy older members not to find their identity in social status and younger people in the congregation not to think that they could find contentment and safety in material things. Edwards applied such discernment and pastoral sensitivity to the problem of lukewarm faith in numerous places in his sermons. He gave nominal Christianity a face and a name, helping his people to identify and counter it in the process.

We must emulate the Northampton pastor and address lukewarm Christianity wherever we find it, including among the young and unmarried, those who are middle-aged, and even older members who belong to the church but know precious little of true Christianity. With young singles, we need to cement the idea that Christianity is not worth the fullness of one's heart and mind because a particular church happens to be cool or interesting, but because it offers them the chance to experience the joys of the cruciform life and the defeat of sin, death, and hell. Christianity is relevant because it is true, not because of its cultural trappings. The gospel offers true delight, true liberation, and true hope as nothing else does. It brings young hearts and minds that hunger for authenticity and beauty into the embrace of the divine.

With middle-aged people who feel stuck in a malaise of life, we need to emphasize the great purpose every life has before God. Christ's redemption, applied to the soul of mankind, will not allow for a half-hearted life, a wasted stewardship of one's talents and abilities. In the gospel, all find significance and purpose, and all find the cure for a lifetime of sins and failures that justly offend a holy God. With older members who may see their membership more as an association than a calling, we must repeatedly go back to basics and teach that Christianity is not a duty to perform or a worthy organization to join. It is an opportunity to die to self, live with the risen Christ, and serve His people. It is altogether different from anything else on this earth. Furthermore, it cannot abide sin, unlike other groups. The call of the gospel necessitates the humiliation of the sinner in which we reckon with our evil and cast ourselves on the mercy of the Son of God.

As we target the temptations of specific groups, we must make sure to instruct parents in our congregations. It is all too easy for our leaders to assume that parents are generally doing well in their rearing of their children and are teaching them biblical truth, modeling godly living, and keeping their kids accountable. In actual fact, we cannot make this assumption. The material in the first chapter shows this in abundance. Where they are not grounded firmly in biblical teaching, parents are often bewildered by the task of Christian discipleship.

If churches desire to win the children of Christian parents, they must train parents to act as agents of vibrant faith. Fathers must embrace their God-given role as familial head; mothers must commit themselves to caring for their children on a daily basis, training them in the things of God. With this setup in place, churches need to promote a model of the family that does not give in to cultural pressures but that emphasizes parental authority, familial cohesiveness, and above all, the transforming power of the gospel.

The Beauty of Christ and the Horror of Sin

*T*he final major focus that we may pick up from Edwards was his theological concern to exalt the beauty of Christ and to unmask the horror of sin. In his preaching and theologizing, Edwards repeatedly placed these parallel ideas at the forefront of his understanding of Christianity. As seen in chapters 2 and 3, he took great care to point out the prevalence of deception even as he detailed the way that the "true sense" of conversion inflamed the penitent heart with love for Christ. Biblical faith, in the end, begins and ends with a simultaneous love for the Savior and a hatred of sin. Without either component, faith never leaves the ground. If we profess to love Jesus Christ but never deal with our sin, we are lost, unforgiven by the Father, and will not enter heaven. If we hate our sin but never run to Christ to receive His atoning grace, we have no remission of sins and we will not see eternal life. The Spirit must propel each of these doctrines into the sinful heart and mind if we are ever to know the grace of God and the glory of true Christianity.

We need to seize these twin emphases in our churches today and make them part of the fabric of our ecclesial life. True Christianity is neither solely sorrow over sin or joy in Christ; it is both, married together, residing in the human heart, which personally receives, believes, and acts on these truths. In churches that all too often drift from these foundational realities to ground their identities in other teachings— whether a political identity, a social cause, or a way of living —we need the dual emphasis on sin's influence and Christ's atonement. Remembering the evil of our depravity and the need to fight it ensures that we will not rest easy in our faith, growing soft and lazy, while rooting ourselves in adoration of Christ warms our hearts to love him and rise above the temptations of this world.

In an age in which we are pressed on every side by challenges and temptations, Christians of all kinds need to go back to the fundamentals and ground their lives and ministries in the glorious person and work of Jesus Christ, fighting sin by focusing on His beauty. We say that our churches are solid, but do our people actually know the gospel? Do they live according to the gospel? Do they love Christ? Do they hate and oppose their sin? This foundational concern must guide our assessment of the health of our congregations and the state of our own souls.

Possible Questions to Ask Our Nominal Friends

*B*efore we conclude, we offer a series of questions that Christians, churches, and pastors may use in conversations with people who profess faith but struggle to commit themselves wholly to the Lord. These questions are not intended to hurt or wound but rather to help nominal Christians discern the true state of their heart in order that they might experience salvation.

Do you love God? In your heart, do you desire to follow Him, worship Him, and obey Him? Does your professed love for God stretch into action? Does it have any practical effect on your life? Would others characterize you as one who loves God? Do you adore God? Do you want to adore Him? (See John 14 for more on this point.)

Do you love the Bible? Do you want to follow the One whom it reveals, Jesus Christ, and follow His commandments? Do you enjoy reading the Bible and take nourishment from it? Do you struggle to read it and possess little desire to obey it? Do you care about the Bible? Do you seek to understand how it should be interpreted, or do you care more about how it fits or does not fit with your natural prejudices and opinions? Do you believe that the Bible is true? Is it all true, or are only parts of it true? (See Psalm 119.)

Do you love living out and sharing the gospel? Do you monetarily support other Christians in need? Do you share the gospel with lost people? Do you care if someone is lost? Is that a concern that comes quickly into your mind when talking with another person? Do you pray much for the salvation of lost sinners? Do you want people to be saved? Do you attempt to live out a Christian life in front of other people? Do you inconvenience yourself to present the gospel to others? Do you suffer in any form for the sake of the gospel? Or is your life free of the sting associated with vibrant Christianity lived out in a pagan world? Do you seek to win family members to Christ? Or do you assume they're fine? Do you ask them penetrating questions or do you simply assume that they are saved? When dealing with others, are spiritual concerns first in your mind? (See Romans 10.)

Do you love Christians? Or are they like any other group of people out there? Does your love take on a practical form? Do you desire to serve other Christians? Do you care when you hear about suffering Christians in other countries? (See 1 John 3.)

Do you enjoy church and draw nourishment from it? Is church endlessly boring to you? Do you like biblical preaching? Do you see the need to be confronted about your sin? Do you avoid church in order to avoid being "judged" or "condemned"? Do you love interaction with other believers? Do you want to support the local church? Do you want to support missionaries? Does the spiritual good of other people concern you? Is it more important for you to do your favorite things on Sunday or to worship God with other believers? Do you continually struggle with finding the motivation to go to church? Do you want to go to church? (See Acts 4.)

Does the matter of eternity concern you? Do you want to go to heaven? Do you not want to go to hell? Do you believe in heaven and hell? If so, does your belief take any actional form? Do you desire to go to heaven to worship God for eternity? Do you want to go to heaven because that's where your favorite people and things are? Do you think about hell? Do you live as if eternity is real? (See Revelation 20.)

Does the Bible shape your ethics and morals? Or do you just go with what you feel at a gut level? When there is conflict between your natural inclinations and what the Bible says, which side wins? Do you ever change your mind as a result of reading the Bible? When making political, ethical, and moral decisions, do you consider scriptural teachings, or do you base your decisions on your moral sense? Do you want the Bible to shape your ethics? Does the Bible affect what you watch, read, and listen to? Do you ever avoid or turn off content that is biblically offensive? Do you care if content is moral or immoral in an explicitly biblical sense? (See 1 John 1.)

If used well, these questions could provide a starting point from which to engage people we love on the question of their Christianity. If we listen well, show empathy, and share the gospel, we may see the Holy Spirit bring true faith to those who desperately need it.

Challenging Nominal Christianity

We began this book with a look at the current state of marriage. We noted, in short, that it has fallen on hard times. We then commented that there is a far deeper form of adultery and half-hearted commitment that plagues our world today —spiritual nominalism. Just as some spouses today go through the motions of marriage, pretending to love the person with whom they have covenanted, some professing Christians join churches without any personal love for the gospel.

This is a hard situation, but the example and teaching of Jonathan Edwards challenge us to press on and to seek true conversion and authentic Christianity in our lives and churches. We desire not to accommodate nominal Christianity—but to address it with the gospel. We seek to call people who profess to love God to do just that: to love Him. If we hope for our world to gain a fresh love for marriage, how much greater is our hope for nominal Christians to truly take Christ as their Lord?

The time is short; the hour draws nearer when the risen King will return to earth and claim His people for Himself. At His coming, He will judge the lukewarm, the nominal believer, spewing them from His mouth, casting them aside. As Edwards did, then, we call to all who will hear to seek the Son while He may be found, to feel the weight of sin's burden, and to cast themselves on the mercy of God. Now, while we still have time, let us prepare ourselves and flee the darkness of this world for the light that will soon break like the dawn.

*T*he preceding has laid out a picture of true Christianity as seen through the eyes of Jonathan Edwards, the Northampton pastor-theologian of eighteenth-century colonial America. Edwards labored in a different era than our own and faced different challenges than we do. Yet as we have seen, in his approach to the problem of nominal Christianity, the pastor sketched out an eminently helpful course to follow. He defined the problem and outlined in his church what listless faith looked like. He also identified the marks of true Christianity, holding up the "true sense" of the gospel as the elemental reality of saving belief. He handed down vivid biographies of two faithful Christians to his people to stoke their faith and show them that they need not be socially eminent or advantaged to win great glory for God. Though his zeal for true Christianity cost him his treasured role and job, he refused to abandon his convictions, showing present-day believers that he lived what he preached.

We who seek to stand for true Christianity in our day can learn much from Edwards. The fight for true Christianity requires, as we have suggested, awareness of our situation, connection to the wisdom of the past (in this case, the wisdom of Edwards on a matter he wrestled with all his life), and a steadfast commitment in our individual and corporate lives to promoting vibrant faith. The fight also depends on our ability to see the horror of our sin and the beauty of Jesus Christ. Only when we understand our depravity and celebrate God's great mercy in Christ will we take seriously the fate of the lost and the state of our churches.

Though Edwards's pastoral career closed on a low note, his fight for true Christianity lives on. This fight began long before he took the Northampton pulpit, and it will continue until the end of the age. In Isaiah, for example, the prophet wrote of a nation stricken with nominalism, lamenting those

> WHO SWEAR BY the name of the Lord
> and confess the God of Israel,
> but not in truth or right. (Isaiah 48:1)

To this same people, God promised in an earlier passage from Isaiah that

> THOUGH YOUR SINS are like scarlet,
>> they shall be as white as snow;
> though they are red like crimson,
>> they shall become like wool. (Isaiah 1:18)

Nominalism is an ancient problem with an ancient solution. The church must turn back to the Lord of the Word. He loves His church (Ephesians 5:25–27). He sustains it by His Spirit, the "Helper" whom Christ spoke of in John 15:26. Though the church struggles, and though it spurns Him as Israel did in former days, yet He will renew it. If Israel would obey the Lord and turn away from temptation and idolatry, the Lord would restore them, as He had done over and over again in the nation's past. In His sovereignty, grace, and undying love for His people, He will do the same in our day.

Acknowledgments

We have a number of people to thank for the production of this volume.

We would like to thank Dave DeWit of Moody Publishers. Dave is an excellent editor and has been a tremendous help and encouragement in all aspects of the process. It was Dave who suggested that this project encompass not one book, but five, forming a comprehensive and definitive introductory series. We are thankful for his vision. We would also thank Chris Reese, who gave excellent feedback on this and every manuscript and made each book clearer and better.

We would like to thank Dr. John Piper for graciously providing a series foreword. It is a signal honor to have Dr. Piper

involved in this project. Dr. Piper has enriched our understanding of Jonathan Edwards as he has for countless people.
We are thankful to the Lord for his ministry, and we deeply
appreciate his commendation of this collection. We are thankful as well for the assistance of David Mathis, Executive Pastoral Assistant to Dr. Piper.

We owe a debt of gratitude to our wives, Bethany Strachan
and Wilma Sweeney. We are grateful for their love and support, without which we could not have written this volume.

We would like to thank good friends who gave encouragement and counsel at various points in the project. Collin
Hansen, Justin Taylor, Ben Peays, Mark Rogers, Andy Naselli,
Jared Compton, Andrew Lisi, Jeremy Treat, Doug Hankins—
thank you.

We thank no one more in an earthly sense than Mark
Dever and Lou Korom. Mark, thank you for your effort to
advance true Christianity and to mentor future pastors. Your
Edwardsean work honors the Lord and will result, we trust, in
a rich reward in the life to come. In the same vein, we honor
Lou Korom, a faithful evangelist. Lou, you have helped so
many others to understand true Christianity. This book is ded-
icated to these faithful servants of Christ.

Above all others, we thank the living Lord of Christianity,
to whom everyone must give an account (Romans 14:12).

Recommended Resources on Jonathan Edwards

*F*or the premier collection of Edwards's own writing, see *The Works of Jonathan Edwards*, vol. 1–26, Yale University Press. Access these works in their entirety free of charge at http://edwards.yale.edu.

For secondary sources, we recommend the following.

Introductory Reading

Byrd, James P. *Jonathan Edwards for Armchair Theologians.* Louisville, KY: Westminster John Knox Press, 2008.

McDermott, Gerald R. *Seeing God: Jonathan Edwards and Spiritual Discernment.* Vancouver: Regent College Publishing, 2000.

Nichols, Stephen A. *Jonathan Edwards: A Guided Tour of His Life and Thought.* Phillipsburg, NJ: Presbyterian & Reformed, 2001.

Storms, Sam. *Signs of the Spirit: An Interpretation of Jonathan Edwards' Religious Affections.* Wheaton, IL: Crossway Books, 2007.

Deeper Reading

Gura, Philip F. *Jonathan Edwards: America's Evangelical.* New York: Hill & Wang, 2005.

Kimnach, Wilson H., Kenneth P. Minkema, and Douglas A. Sweeney, eds. *The Sermons of Jonathan Edwards: A Reader.* New Haven: Yale University Press, 1999.

Lesser, M. X. *Reading Jonathan Edwards: An Annotated Bibliography in Three Parts, 1729–2005.* Grand Rapids: Eerdmans, 2008

Marsden, George. *Jonathan Edwards: A Life.* New Haven: Yale University Press, 2003.

McDermott, Gerald R., ed. *Understanding Jonathan Edwards: An Introduction to America's Theologian.* New York: Oxford University Press, 2009.

Moody, Josh. *The God-Centered Life: Insights from Jonathan Edwards for Today.* Vancouver: Regent College Publishing, 2007.

Murray, Iain H. *Jonathan Edwards: A New Biography.* Edinburgh: Banner of Truth Trust, 1987.

Piper, John. *God's Passion for His Glory: Living the Vision of Jonathan Edwards.* Wheaton, IL: Crossway Books, 1998.

_____, and Justin Taylor, eds. *A God Entranced Vision of All Things: The Legacy of Jonathan Edwards.* Wheaton, IL: Crossway Books, 2004.

Smith, John E., Harry S. Stout, and Kenneth P. Minkema, eds. *A Jonathan Edwards Reader.* New Haven: Yale University Press, 1995.

Sweeney, Douglas A. *Jonathan Edwards and the Ministry of the Word: A Model of Faith and Thought.* Downers Grove, IL: InterVarsity Press, 2009.

BRINGING YOU THE TIMELESS CLASSICS

Classics

Selected for their enduring influence and timeless perspective ...

Answers to Prayer
ISBN-13: 978-0-8024-5650-2

The Confessions
of St. Augustine
ISBN-13: 978-0-8024-5651-9

How to Pray
ISBN-13: 978-0-8024-5652-6

The Imitation of Christ
ISBN-13: 978-0-8024-5653-3

The Pilgrim's Progress
ISBN-13: 978-0-8024-5654-0

The True Vine
ISBN-13: 978-0-8024-5655-7

Power Through Prayer
ISBN-13: 978-0-8024-5662-5

The Christian's Secret
of a Happy Life
ISBN-13: 978-0-8024-5656-4

Hudson Taylor's
Spiritual Secret
ISBN-13: 978-0-8024-5658-8

MOODY
PUBLISHERS
MoodyClassics.com

BRINGING YOU THE TIMELESS CLASSICS

Classics

... these are key books that every believer on the journey of spiritual formation should read.

Holiness
ISBN-13: 978-0-8024-5455-3

Born Crucified
ISBN-13: 978-0-8024-5456-0

Names of God
ISBN-13: 978-0-8024-5856-8

The Overcoming Life
ISBN-13: 978-0-8024-5451-5

All of Grace
ISBN-13: 978-0-8024-5452-2

The Secret
of Guidance
ISBN-13: 978-0-8024-5454-6

The Incomparable Christ
ISBN-13: 978-0-8024-5660-1

Orthodoxy
ISBN-13: 978-0-8024-5657-1

The Apostolic Fathers
ISBN-13: 978-0-8024-5659-5

MOODY
PUBLISHERS
MoodyClassics.com

BV 4520 .S68 2010
Strachan, Owen.
Jonathan Edwards on true
 Christianity